Tables of Content

Tables of Content

by

*Eleanor Graves and
Ralph Graves*

✳

*Picture Editor:
Mindy Clay*

Crown Publishers, Inc.
New York

Page ii: Top photograph by Alex McLean; center left photograph of Norris Church Mailer in a dress designed by Arnold Scaasi by William Waldron; center right photograph by Bill Helms; bottom photograph by Terry Gruber.

Page 3, bottom: Bill Cunningham

Page 8: Portrait of Caroline Schermerhorn Astor: Courtesy of The Metropolitan Museum of Art, Gift of R. Thornton Wilson and Orme Wilson.

Page 8: C. K. G. Billings Horseback Dinner at Sherrys: Courtesy of Museum of the City of New York, The Byron Collection.

Pages 8–9: Photos of fancy dress balls: From the Collections of the General Research Division, The New York Public Library, Astor, Lenox and Tilden Foundations.

Page 9: Mrs. W. K. Vanderbilt at fancy dress ball: Courtesty of UPI/BETTMANN.

Page 77: Jeanne Trudeau

Braised spinach (page 87), Mushroom Duxelles (page 87), Rice Soubise (page 88), and Caramelized Pear Tarts (page 89) are from The Way To Cook by Julia Child. Copyright © 1989 by Julia Child. Reprinted by permission of Alfred A. Knopf, Inc.

Braised Saddle of Veal (page 85) was specially created by Julia Child for the Tables of Content dinner.

The publisher gratefully acknowledges permission to reprint from the following: "All That and Heaven Too? The Marriage of Society and Charity," copyright © 1993 by Barbara Goldsmith; "Dinner at the Round Table," copyright © 1993 by Brendan Gill; "Pretty Decent Chinese Takeout" copyright © 1992 by Calvin Trillin.

Published by Crown Publishers, Inc., 201 East 50th Street, New York, New York 10022.

Member of the Crown Publishing Group.

Random House, Inc., New York, Toronto, London, Sydney, Auckland.

CROWN is a trademark of Crown Publishers, Inc.

Manufactured in Japan

Designed by Linda Kocur

Library of Congress Cataloging-in-Publication Data

Graves, Ralph.

Tables of content /Ralph and Eleanor Graves. — 1st ed.

Includes index.

1. New York Public Library—Finance. 2. Library fund raising—New York (N.Y.) 3. Dinners and dining—New York (N.Y.) I. Graves, Eleanor. II. Title.

Z733.N63G73 1993

027.4747'1—dc20   92-31157 CIP

ISBN 0-517-59093-X

10 9 8 7 6 5 4 3 2 1

First Edition

contents

acknowledgments

This book was conceived, created, and edited, as a personal contribution to the Library, by Eleanor Graves, former executive editor of *Life,* and by Ralph Graves, former managing editor of *Life.* The book could not have happened without them.

The major articles were written, as a personal contribution to the Library, by Brendan Gill, Barbara Goldsmith, and Calvin Trillin. All are longtime supporters of the Library.

In addition to being cochairman and a hostess for all five "chapters" of the Tables of Content dinners, Sonny Sloan has been a major factor at the Library behind the development of this book, and she merits special recognition and thanks.

There was space in the book to report on and show only nineteen of the fifty-five dinners held in 1991. The Library appreciates the eyewitness descriptions of those nineteen dinners contributed by hosts, hostesses, guests, or friends.

The film for the photographs taken for the book was contributed by Eastman Kodak. The film was developed, processed, and printed as a contribution by the Time-Life Photo Lab. The Library is grateful to both organizations for their generosity.

Without Barbara Fleischman to start it all, there would have been no Tables of Content dinners. The Library is grateful to her and all the hosts and hostesses who volunteered to give one or more dinners over the past decade and to the many people who volunteered to be speakers or entertainers at those dinners. A complete list of those who have been involved appears on pages 172 to 179. In addition, a special word of thanks to Fern Schad, who provided invaluable research and organization in arranging the Tables of Content dinners.

Elizabeth Cahill
Director of External Affairs
The New York Public Library

introduction

by

Timothy S. Healy

**President, The New York
Public Library***

Of all The New York Public Library's holdings, the manuscript most frequently consulted, I was recently told, is a recipe for "small beer," recorded in George Washington's own hand in *Notebooks of a Virginia Colonel*. Although the association between the father of our country and food and beverage may come as a surprise, The New York Public Library's culinary collection is an outstanding archive, spanning the entire globe, with items in some 300 different languages and dialects. The Library's catalogs reveal over 14,000 individual items under the heading "Cookery" alone, from "Cookery, Afghan" to "Cookery, Zucchini," with sections on cake, camp, and "at sea."

The Rare Book Room houses the first printed cookbook, Platina's *De Honesta Voluptate*, published in Venice in 1475.

*Timothy Healy was President of the Library until his death in December 1992.

Other classics include Amelia Simmons's *American Cookery* (1796), Hannah Glasse's *The Art of Cookery, Made Plain and Easy* (1747), and what could best be described as the *Joy of Cooking* of the mid-nineteenth century, Mrs. Beeton's *Book of Household Management*, published in 1859–1861 and preserved in its original twenty-four parts in the Arents Collection.

There are also rare items, things that catch one's eye for their oddity but have their own regional and historical importance. In The Schomburg Center for Research in Black Culture is the first commercially published book by a black American, Robert Roberts's *House Servants' Directory or a Monitor for Private Families* (1827). It contains practical hints on marketing, carving, even a formula for turning "good wine into vinegar in three hours," and, more practical still, one for returning "that same wine to its first taste." From another era and across the world is *What to Tell the Cook; Or, the Native Cook's Assistant, Being a Choice Collection . . . in English and Tamil*. And what will future generations make of Bobby Seale's *Barbecue'n with Bobby* (1988), T. Edwin Belt's *Wild*

Plants for Wine Making, or Lyn Stallworth and Rod Kennedy Jr.'s *The Brooklyn Cookbook* (1991)?

menus give an incomparable view of society and culture, and the Library's collections contain bills of fare from 15¢ lunchrooms as well as such turn-of-the-century restaurants as the Café des Beaux Arts (located at Bryant Park South), Fifth Avenue's Delmonico's, the Dakota (in the landmark building), and the Waldorf (home of the dubious salad), and, to our shame, the Maceo Hotel Restaurant on West Fifty-third Street, "for colored people only." The prices at the Hotel Claremont in New York are reminders of thriftier days. Lobster Newburg cost 75¢, prime ribs of beef a modest 60¢, while a boy out to impress his girl could order chateaubriand for $2.00. A modest bottle of Médoc could be purchased for $1.00, while, for big spenders, Château Lafite was priced at a clearly extravagant $4.50. For those in a mood to celebrate, a bottle of extra dry Mumm's cost $3.50.

Some menus are interesting not just for what was being served but because of the guest list. For instance, we can find out who sat next to the Prince of Wales (Edward VII) at one banquet, or who was on the dais at a luncheon tendered to Colonel John Glenn and his fellow astronauts. These lists are delightfully illustrated and gossipy, and they tell us a great deal about the taste and style of a period: about how the good life was perceived at those vast Victorian club dinners or, indeed, at the Table Royal of Charles II.

The New York Public Library's *Tables of Content* partakes of both charms and contains the same kind of detailed and precise grasp of a moment in time. This book not only celebrates the Library's innovative and successful fund-raising venture but also gives recipes, menus, table settings, flower arrangements, music, and details on wines (although, to the best of my knowledge, no host poured the modern equivalent of small beer). For instance, it tells us how Mr. and Mrs. Richard Scurry, Jr., managed to recapture Victorian times with guests clad in Victorian finery and with such details as tulips and hyacinths in the greenhouse; that Joanna and Daniel Rose, in celebrating Edward VII, served a Madeira from their father's cellar that had, according to the custom of the time, been back and forth to India; and that Sonny Sloan has a peerless collection of red glass, to say nothing of a regal bearded collie named Elizabeth.

Former Chairman of the Board Richard Salomon and his wife, Edna, used the title "Living Well Is the Best Revenge" for their 1983 Tables of Content dinner. That dinner really started the ball rolling, and began a fund-raising activity for the Library that has been enormously successful. The generous hosts and hostesses meet all the costs of the dinner, and thus the "board-fee" asked of guests puts the Library in the enviable position where gross is net, where all the gifts support the purchase, cataloging, and servicing of books in the Library's collections.

hosts, special guests, chefs, and diners—almost a thousand people participated in each of the five evenings. Hosts and guests were pleased to contribute to the Library and to be involved in an event that was such varied fun. Where else might you be asked to wear magical costume, Belle Epoque garb, a Roman toga, bridal attire (to celebrate Madame Bovary's wedding), or to dress like a 1920s gun moll? Just as the Library's culinary resources cover every part of the globe, so have the dinners, which have featured the cuisines of Spain, Japan, Portugal, France, India, Tangiers, Rio, Old Havana, Russia, California, New Orleans, and Indonesia. One dinner offered a salad of wild greens from Queens and a mustard dressing of Bronx herbs. Course after course was prepared by such stars of the culinary firmament as Craig Claiborne, Susan and Barry Wine, Edward Giobbi, Julie Sahni, Christopher Idone, and Ken Hom. Guests of honor have included Cy Coleman, Nien Cheng, David Halberstam, Tom Wolfe, and Sidney Sheldon. Unavoidably absent, a number of friends still made their presence felt, including Czar Nicholas and Czarina Alexandra, Thomas Jefferson, Peggy Guggenheim, James Bond, Walter Lippmann, "Lucy" Australopithecus, and Louis the Beloved of eighteenth-century France.

There is another purpose to this book. It puts in tangible form the Library's "thank you" to all who hosted these evenings and to all who came. Among them they raised many thousands of dollars to expand and deepen our collections, and to remind New Yorkers of the Library's importance in the life of the city. To all these benefactors the Library says cheers, *prosit, salud, pesetas y amor, santé,* and *l'chaim.*

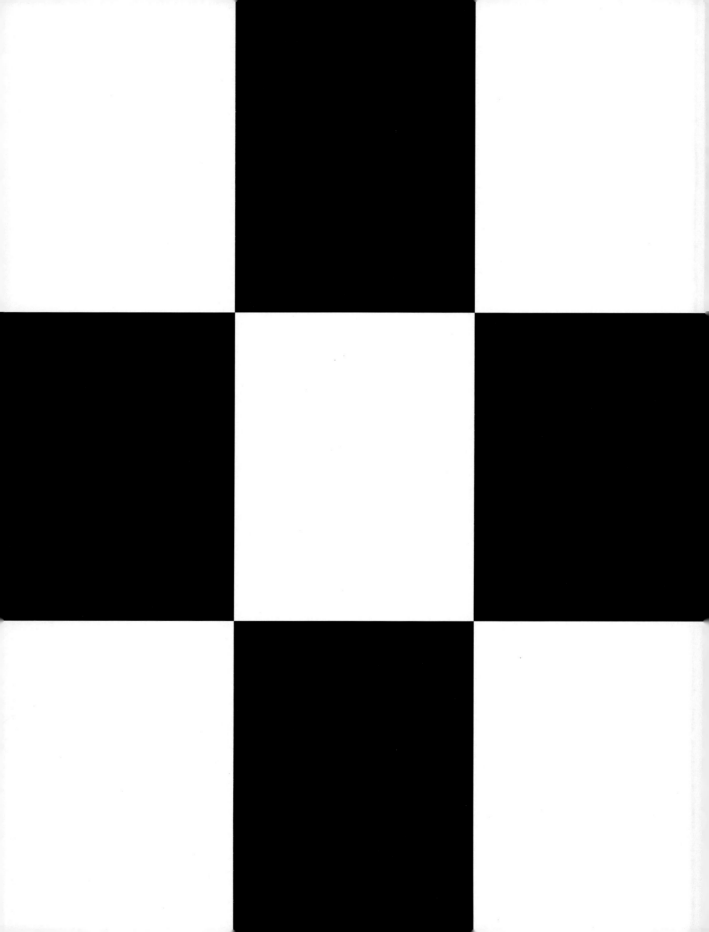

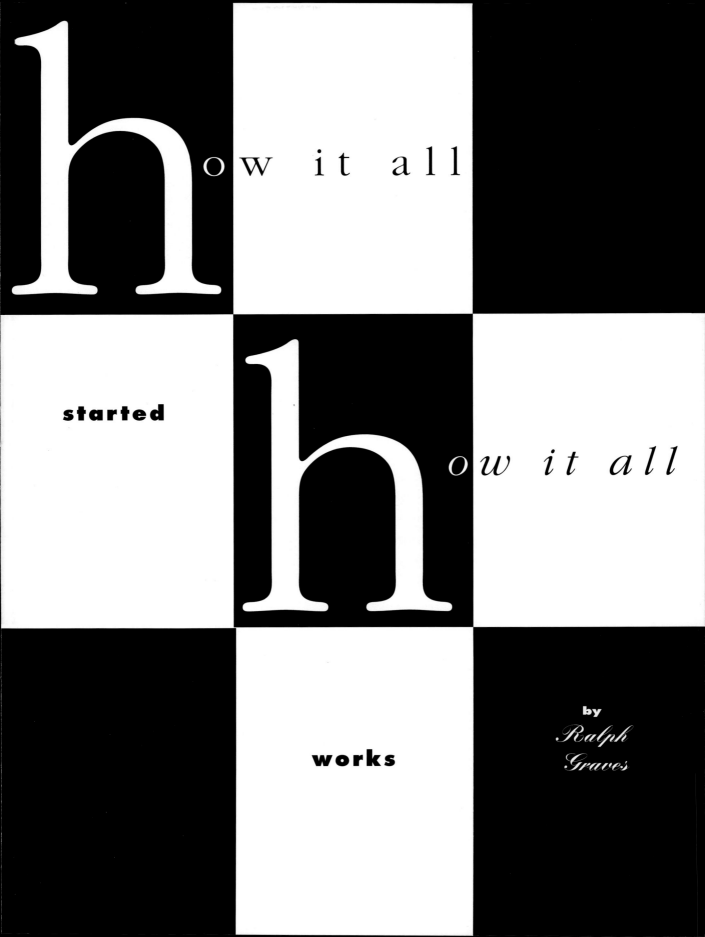

how it all

started

how it all

how it all

works

by
Ralph
Graves

most successful ideas have cloudy origins and multiple authors. But everyone agrees on how Tables of Content began.

In early 1982 Barbara Fleischman, an ardent supporter and volunteer worker for the Library, accompanied her husband, Larry, to Oklahoma City, where he was going to make a speech at the Oklahoma Art Center. While her husband and the museum director discussed details, Barbara was handed a cookbook.

"Everybody knows my penchant for cookbooks," she says. "I have hundreds of them. When I opened this cookbook, I saw that it was a little offbeat."

The director explained that in order to raise money for the art center, eighteen or twenty people gave a theme dinner on the same night every year—a French dinner, an Italian dinner, and so on—and the guests paid to attend. After a few successful years, the art center decided to make a cookbook out of the best recipes, and it had sold quite well at the museum shop.

"I told my husband," Barbara Fleischman says, "that this idea—fund-raising theme dinners—was made for New York. We come from Detroit, and I'm used to people telling me, 'That will *never* fly in New York.' But I'm not easily daunted. When we got back to New York, I told Andrew Heiskell, the chairman of the Library's Board of Trustees, what I wanted to do. I said I wanted to have as many as a hundred dinners on one night, and they should all have literary themes to celebrate the Library. At that time, I was president of the Friends of the Library, so he gave me permission to try it. A long time later he told me his first thought was, 'This woman is off the wall.' "

Barbara Fleischman gathered a committee of interested people, including Sonny Sloan, who became cochair, and then a group of advisers who knew a lot about food and dinners. Sue Mueller, another volunteer activist, came up with the title, Tables of Content.

"We followed Oklahoma's lead from the start," Barbara Fleischman says. "Everybody had a friend or several friends who might be willing to give a dinner for the Library. When it came to inviting guests, we were very careful about security. We didn't want total strangers coming into people's homes, so we vetted every person who would receive an invitation. There are cranks, you know. So we had no advertising, no publicity. Everything was strictly by invitation. I started out with the hope of giving one hundred dinners, all on the same night, but in the end it shrank down to ninety-two or ninety-three. Not too bad for an idea that would 'never fly in New York.' "

by 1983, the year of the first dinner, the cost of a ticket to a New York City charity affair had risen spectacularly. There were many $500 and $1,000 nights. Barbara Fleischman wanted to reach out to all the people who couldn't afford the big benefits but who might enjoy a good evening for a worthy cause at a low price. The 1983 ticket was only $150 a person. Even today, after ten years of inflation, the price is only $350.

t his is how the finances work: Each host or hostess contributes the cost of the dinner itself, for which they are entitled to take a tax deduction as a charitable contribution to the Library. Each paying guest is entitled to a partial tax deduction for the cost of the ticket. All the money paid by all the guests goes to the Library.

"The beauty of the thing," says Barbara Fleischman, "is that there is very little expense to the Library. We pay for the cost of the original invitation, which is quite elaborate, and for the various mailings and phone calls and for a little extra staff help. I don't like to be involved in any charity event where the cost is too high. Some charity events, especially charity balls, can have costs of fifty percent or even seventy-five percent of what you take in. I hate that."

The biggest problem Tables of Content has to face is the question of who gets to go to which dinner. Months before the night of the dinners, the Library mails out an invitation to each potential guest, listing all the dinners, the hosts and hostesses, the theme of each party, and the dress code (black tie, festive, informal, or costume). Each poten-

Barbara Fleischman, top, is founder of the Tables of Content dinners. She had the original idea and she has been an active and caring contributor ever since. Sonny Sloan, above, has been co-chair from the beginning.

tial guest is asked to list, in order of preference, the six dinners he or she would most like to attend. So far, so good.

however, some parties turn out to be much more popular than others and are oversubscribed. Sometimes guests who don't get into their first-choice dinner are annoyed. Barbara Fleischman remembers one couple in the early days who didn't get into their first-choice dinner but simply showed up anyway, much to the dismay of the host and hostess.

Nor is this a one-way street. Most people who volunteer to give Tables of Content dinners simply love to entertain in a lavish and imaginative way, and they cheerfully accept whatever guests are assigned to them. But a few hosts and hostesses, after agreeing to put on a splendid entertainment in their own homes, are bothered if they wind up with a guest list that is not chock-full of celebrities.

A still worse thing can happen. New Yorkers are quirky and fickle people. One year everybody signs up for parties featuring pianists. The next time around, nobody cares in the least about pianists but is crazy about sopranos. Tables of Content does its best to catch the current trends and to plan accordingly, but New Yorkers are so unpredictable that an attractive-sounding dinner can wind up with almost no subscribers. Since it would not be worthwhile to give such a dinner, the Library has the painful job of telling the host or hostess that

no one wants to come to their nice party and that it has to be canceled. This is a blow to self-esteem, of course, but after a very sad gulp, most people manage to survive and even volunteer to give another, more popular dinner the next time around.

"The thing I discovered," says Barbara Fleischman, "was that the best thing to do is to be diplomatic. After all, it's in a very good cause, and the thing to do is to try to keep everybody happy and make it work." It usually does.

After the first two dinners in 1983 and 1985, Barbara Fleischman resigned from Tables of Content. Her cochair, Sonny Sloan, has run it ever since, first with Mrs. Samuel C. Butler and Mrs. James Hoge as her cochairs and then in 1991 with a full committee.

Sonny Sloan is one of the handful of hostesses who has given a Tables of Content dinner all five times, and of course she has worked on the arrangements for all the dinners every year. She has developed her own guidelines for what will work and what won't, and she advises the hosts and hostesses accordingly. "A private home or apartment is much better than a restaurant," she says. "After all, the guests can go to any restaurant any time they want to. You have to give them something different." She also thinks it is vital to offer some kind of special entertainment—often a speaker, often a singer. "New Yorkers require this," she says. Although a few rare dinners for as many as fifty guests have been successful, she thinks smaller is better. "The ideal is anywhere between twelve and twenty."

Her favorite among her own dinner parties broke this last rule. It was called a Black-and-White Dinner Dance because that is what the thirty-five guests were told to wear. Black-and-white television sets all around the dance floor played continuous tapes of Fred Astaire's and Ginger Rogers's best numbers from their best movies. "Nobody wanted to go home," Sonny remembers.

Many other memorable dinners have also been given. To mention just a few:

• In 1987 for her Anna Karenina dinner, Mona Riklis Ackerman had waiters dressed as Russian guards stationed at the entrance to her ballroom. The women received a dance card and a fan, and all the men received medals. All guests were photographed with a pair of Russian wolfhounds.

• In 1989 Hilary and Stuart Oran gave an Eighteenth-Century American Antiques dinner. It opened at Bernard Levy and S. Dean Antiques with champagne cocktails and a guided tour. Then the sixteen guests piled into horse-drawn carriages and clip-clopped down Park Avenue to the Orans' apartment, where they were greeted by a Colonial Dame in eighteenth-century costume. At each guest's dinner place, to be taken home as a keepsake, was a dollhouse-size diorama of a notable person in American history: Betsy Ross, Paul Revere, Thomas Jefferson, George Washington, Dolley Madison.

• In 1983 Julia and Carter Walker gave an American Indian dinner. As a board member of the Museum of the American Indian, she did research in the museum's library and, with the help of chef Barbara Gorin, came up with an authentic and most unusual menu. It included yellow squash soup with toasted sunflower and pumpkin seeds, blue corn bread with herb butter, juniper berry lamb stew with corn dumplings, and Navajo feast day cookies with black walnuts. Having thought up this exotic feast, Julia Walker decided that her New York City living room lacked the proper ambience. She and her husband brought down their collection of Indian rugs from their Adirondacks camp and "with *great* flair" strewed them over the chintz couches, brocade loveseats, and comfy chairs. "To my horror," Julia Walker recalls, "our living room ended up looking like a high-class Southwestern bordello." But since the guests seemed not to make this connection, the dinner was a great success.

• In 1989 Mr. and Mrs. William Knowles hired the American Symphony Orchestra for the evening, and every guest had a chance to conduct the orchestra in his or her best "Dreams of Glory" style.

• In 1985 Alan and Hannah Pakula put on An Aphrodisiac Feast, with literary

sources for each course: oysters on the half shell ("Oysters are amatory food."—Byron, *Don Juan*); champagne ("A woman in her cups has no defense/As lechers know from long experience."—Chaucer, *Canterbury Tales*); salmon mousse with shrimp ("We have observed that those who live almost entirely on shellfish and fish . . . are more ardent in love than all others."—Venette, *Tableau de l'Amour Conjugal*); small birds ("A sparrow baked and given to a woman in her drink will make her dissolve and melt away for love."—Cyranus, *Magick of Kirani*). The Pakulas' menu footnote pointed out that "Cornish game hens were substituted for sparrows, which were not available on the market today."

Sonny Sloan, left, papers in hand, briefs future hosts and hostesses of Tables of Content dinners on what to expect. Mrs. Sloan should know—she has been a hostess herself for all five years that the dinners have been held, in addition to being chief strategist and cheerleader.

Most Tables of Content hosts and hostesses think up their own themes for their dinners, but they have to think them up by the first week of June so that the elaborate invitation can be designed and printed and mailed out on time. There is invariably a lot of last-minute scurrying around.

The Tables of Content dinners not only make money for the Library but make new friends as well. Some guests enjoy their dinner so much that they volunteer to give a dinner of their own the next time around. Some guests are so impressed by the quality of the event that they make an additional contribution to the Library.

Still, accidents do happen. In 1991 Alexander Cohen, television and theatre producer, volunteered to give a party for fourteen people with charades after dinner. On the evening of December 11, while he and his wife, Hildy, were out at a cocktail party, his assistant, Jenny Ober, was in the Cohens' apartment making apple pies for tomorrow night's gala dinner. She was dressed in jogging clothes and sneakers and was covered with flour when the doorbell rang. The Cohens had mixed up the date. Fourteen people were arriving *right now* for dinner.

Jenny located the Cohens at their cocktail party, gave them the ghastly news, and then, still covered with flour, stalled the guests with glasses of champagne. The Cohens raced home, canceled the dinner party they were supposed to attend (much

to the annoyance of their hostess), and took their guests out to dinner at the Raphael restaurant next door. Fortunately the owner was a close friend who managed to crowd three tables together and seat them all. Everybody was a good sport and everybody had more champagne. Finally one guest asked, "What are you going to do with all that food you have for tomorrow night?" "I don't know," Hildy Cohen said. "Why don't you come back tomorrow night and help us eat it?" Which is just what they all did.

"That," says Barbara Fleischman, "is class."

Photograph by Martha Holmes

all that

and heaven

too?

The Marriage of Society and Charity

by

Barbara Goldsmith

Barbara Goldsmith, best-selling author and social historian, tells how society and charity melded a century ago. She is a Trustee of the Library, where she specializes in paper conservation and preservation.

at breakfast one morning in the winter of 1896, Mrs. Bradley Martin, daughter of Andrew Carnegie's partner Henry Phipps, upon reading in her daily newspaper that millions of working-class Americans depended on soup kitchens and other charities and that thousands of New Yorkers were close to starvation, had a sudden whim. She leaned across the table and announced to her husband that she would hold a costume ball, "to give an impetus to trade." At least that's how she explained it afterward, when she was pressed to justify what turned out to be in today's currency a $3 million party. The 1880s, like the 1980s, had been a time of gross affluence, but in 1892 the market had fallen steeply. More than 15,000 businesses failed and 600 banks closed their doors. Over the next four years there was no recovery in sight.

Since the Bradley Martins' main residence was in London and their New York brownstone was too small, they chose for their party the Grand Ballroom of the Waldorf Astoria Hotel (the name Waldorf having derived from the town in Germany where the father of John Jacob Astor owned a butcher shop). Newspaper reporters avidly covered every detail of the impending "fancy dress fete," from the cartloads of white orchids at $2 apiece, to the couturiers' sketches of $10 thousand costumes, to the wildly extravagant jewelry: Mrs. Bradley Martin and her husband, seemingly unaware of the risk they were taking, or the irony involved, confided to the press that she planned to wear a ruby necklace that once had belonged to Queen Marie Antoinette and that he would attend as Louis XV.

Soon after this announcement, death threats began to arrive at the Bradley Martin brownstone on Twentieth Street and Fifth Avenue. Anarchists were caught planting a bomb under the house. Another group of anarchists announced that they planned to throw bombs through the windows of the Waldorf during the ball. On the night of the ball, guests arrived to find the hotel windows boarded up. Three hundred policemen supervised by Theodore Roosevelt, assistant police commissioner of New York City, patrolled Fifth Avenue outside the Waldorf. Ninety Pinkerton detectives stationed themselves around the perimeter of the ballroom, no doubt spoiling the carefully and expensively created illusion of Versailles.

The American clergy, as the representatives of God, found in the Bradley Martin ball a morality tale. Dr. William Rainsford, rector of New York's St. George's Church, warned that the Bradley Martin fete would "draw attention to the growing gulf which separates the rich and poor and serves to increase the discontent of the latter." The

Reverend Madison Peters, in a sermon entitled "The Use and Misuse of Wealth," said of the ball, "Sedition is born in the lap of such luxury—so fell Rome, Thebes, Babylon, and Carthage."

The lesson had become clear: In the face of enormous wealth juxtaposed against abject poverty, extravagant entertainments needed a reason for being. Because of the need to justify its excesses, American society formed an uneasy marriage with charity.

long before the Civil War had turned America upside down, a stern Calvinism had dominated American life. In the early 1800s Lyman Beecher had preached his doctrine in a whitewashed church in East Hampton. His salary was $300 a year and from that he bought his wife, Roxana, the mother of five and schoolmistress to twenty more, a bale of cotton. The enterprising Roxana sat up many a night spinning, weaving, and braiding the cotton into a carpet on which she painted a floral border with colors of her own grinding and mixing. Roxana then "adorned her wooden chairs with patterns of silver and gilt." The East Hampton town fathers were appalled at this display on the part of a preacher's wife, and soon a deacon appeared in the Beechers' parlor, looked around, and asked tartly, "Think you can have all that, and *Heaven too?*"

How different from Lyman Beecher was his son, Henry Ward Beecher, who by the mid-1860s was the most famous preacher in America. Every Sunday Henry Ward Beecher bellowed out his Gospel of Love to more than a thousand congregants at Brooklyn's Plymouth Church as he extolled worldly wealth, grandeur, and self-indulgence. Beecher gazed out at his congregation and cried in exaltation, "You are crystalline. Your faces are radiant. . . . Ye are gods!" And indeed they were gods, these new titans who made and broke the rules as they went along.

In these churches reposed the conscience of American society. Other denominations, Catholics and Jews, were excluded. The church suited the times, and offered as a sop to worldly ambition and greed the easy penance of charity, one that appealed to American businessmen who did not have far to look in order to remember what poverty was like.

In primitive societies, actual sacrifices to the gods are integral to the rituals of enjoyment, and in more sophisticated ones, symbolic sacrifices are mandated. The arrangement seemed equitable: parting with a bit of wealth in exchange for a clear conscience. William Lawrence, first Episcopal Bishop of Massachusetts, declared that a millionaire who gave to charity was as close to Christ's bosom as Saint Paul or Saint Francis of Assisi. "Material prosperity is helping to make the national character sweeter, more joyous, more unselfish, more Christlike," he said. As social historian Dixon Wecter observed, "American philanthropy emanates from a kind of puritanic malaise seeking to justify its wealth in the sight of envious man and a retributive God."

at today's charity events the themes, the dress, the food, the entertainment all reflect trace memories of social patterns formed an American century ago, patterns that have since crystallized, often producing odd anomalies. Consider the rituals that encourage us to succumb to extravagantly rich food that we would never eat at home. Consider how eagerly we reach for the favors, often a glossy-black miniature shopping bag stuffed with magenta tissue paper, containing cologne or a scarf. Consider the charity event that so distorts content that at a PEN benefit one snatches a miniature potato stuffed with beluga caviar from a silver platter garnished with *real* books sprayed with gold glitter. At a Belle Epoque ten-course banquet to benefit City Meals On Wheels, at tables set with crisp Porthault linen, votive candles, and a profusion of spring flowers, one can feast conscience free on foie gras and pressed duck, knowing that part of the price of a ticket will pay for a hot meal delivered daily to one of New York's incapacitated elderly citizens.

The psychological agenda behind these parties is obvious: Outward forms may alter but motivations remain the same. In affluent decades, displays of wealth escalate and even in poorer decades like the present one, these habits persist. But in our present shaky economy "conspicuous consumption" is risky. Right now those plover egg-sized diamonds of the Gilded Age and the 1980s remain in the vault. Too vulgar? No, too dangerous. "Remember, darling, they cut off her finger to get the ring."

American society as we know it today, that half of the marriage, began to emerge directly after the Civil War, when most of the guideposts to a stable world had been ripped away. There was a quick reshuffle and men who had been tinkers, hod carriers, stevedores, and farmers before the Great Rebellion flocked to New York with their newly plundered wealth and their socially ambitious wives who, according to social historian Thomas Beer, lived "in a state of domestic prudery and rampant rapacity." Typical of this group was Darius Ogden Mills, a former shopkeeper who struck it rich in California gold. He arrived in Gotham one morning, plunked down today's equivalent of $7 million for a plot of land on Fifty-first Street and Fifth Avenue, left for an eight-month trip, and returned to find his new home completely decorated and fully staffed. The furnishings alone cost today's equivalent of $8 million.

There they were, this group of parvenus, poised to indulge their new leisure and celebrate their new status through entry into the closely guarded bastion of society ruled by Caroline Schermerhorn Astor (picture on page 8), *the* Mrs. Astor of the day. Perhaps in compensation for her relationship with her unfaithful, indifferent, and frequently absent husband, William

Astor, Jr., his wife devoted her energies to becoming the undisputed queen of so-called society. The ballroom of her Thirty-fourth Street brownstone could accommodate four hundred guests and they became, as we know, the socially anointed.

The formula for social success still followed today, however, was not invented by Mrs. Astor but by Alva Vanderbilt (picture on page 9). Plump, pugnacious Alva, wife of William K. Vanderbilt and daughter-in-law of the Commodore, was a woman of determination. When she arranged for her daughter Consuelo to marry the Duke of Marlborough, Alva promised him a fortune and locked her reluctant daughter in her bedroom until she consented.

To Mrs. Astor the Vanderbilts were arrivistes, although in quick-moving New York society the only real difference between a Vanderbilt and an Astor was one generation. William Astor's grandfather John Jacob had been known to eat peas and ice cream off his knife blade; at the Albert Gallatins' dinner table, he wiped his greasy fingers on the white dress of their daughter. Still, a generation later, the crude living presence of Commodore Vanderbilt was unacceptable to Mrs. Astor. The Commodore's speech was coarse, his profanity spectacular; he chewed tobacco and spat it onto his hostesses' Persian carpets. Luckily for his daughter-in-law Alva, the Commodore died in 1877 and the memory of his behavior was fading four years later when she began to plan her social conquest of Mrs. Astor.

Alva Vanderbilt invented the social formula that has been followed with variations ever since. The formula succeeds even today because she intuitively understood what appeals to the American social psyche. She provided an irresistible venue for entertaining by commissioning a Fifth Avenue château that might have been plucked from the Loire valley. She arranged a ball for twelve hundred, two years in the planning. She engaged a brigade of chefs imported from Paris, and a regiment of ladies' maids, butlers, waiters, and footmen to attend her guests. And Alva's party favors were worth scrambling for: twenty-four-carat gold combs, rings and compacts set with rubies and diamonds, and for the men, gold and ruby cuff links.

After Alva's ball, during the last decade of the nineteenth century, favor mania escalated. One Newport dinner featured unset diamonds, rubies, and sapphires hidden beneath sand in the center of the table. At each place was a silver pail and shovel and at a signal the guests dug for treasure. At one New York dinner, the favors were diamond and gold bracelets wrapped in the dinner napkins; at another, gold oysters contained real South Sea pearls. Once in a-while there was a maverick: the antic Mrs. W. E. D. Stokes presented the gentlemen at her dinner party with live bullfrogs, some of which promptly escaped from their baskets and jumped onto plates and into wineglasses.

alva set the style: She ordered costumes from the Paris couturiers Worth and Pacquin (today's equivalent of the anointed Scaasi, Oscar de la Renta, and Bill Blass). Her florist provided today's equivalent of a million dollars' worth of flowers. Social critic Thorstein Veblen noted that when American hostesses entertained, orchids, "being the most costly of flowers, were introduced in profusion." The Vanderbilts' entire third-floor gymnasium (yes, Virginia, they had such a room in those days) was decorated with "trees" of white orchids, which became Alva's signature flower. Nothing changes. Veblen, as if he were here today, also wrote that social display took place by introducing "incredible viands and beverages. . . trinkets. . . seemly apparel and architecture. . . games, dances, and narcotics."

The Vanderbilt ball seemed irresistible, and both Mrs. Astor and her daughter Carrie were *not* invited. Caroline Schermerhorn Astor dispatched Ward McAllister to straighten things out with Mrs. Vanderbilt. (McAllister was to Mrs. Astor roughly what Jerry Zipkin was to First Lady Nancy Reagan, an acerbic arbiter elegantiarum. Someone who remarks, "My dear, those shoes—they won't do! And that purse!") Upon receiving McAllister, Alva Vanderbilt expressed mock distress. "But how can I invite them?" she asked.

"Neither Mrs. Astor nor Miss Astor has ever called on me."

The following afternoon Caroline Schermerhorn Astor presented her calling card at the Vanderbilt mansion. The card read simply "Mrs. Astor." Prefixes were as unnecessary then, as suffixes are today (as anyone knows who has dropped the name Brooke). The Astor invitations were promptly dispatched.

Without a doubt, American society, as we know it, was the creation of women. Behavioral therapist Kenneth Greenspan points out why this is so: "On the most primitive level, men are hunters and warriors. They bond with other males and go out into the world to assert their supremacy. Women are nesters: to them falls the propagation, education, and guidance of the species."

These primitive roles help explain why, for more than a century, American men have consistently complained about society dinners but once there frequently enjoy the status of being with powerful, successful fellow males. Victorian gentlemen reluctantly endured formal dinners after which they promptly departed to the club or the brothel, a convention to which Henry James delicately alluded when he wrote of the American society dinner: "There was nothing for us to do at eleven o'clock—or for the *ladies* at least—but to scatter or go to bed."

And society dinners fulfilled other primitive needs as well. Anthropologist Lionel Tiger says, "The need to eat in company is basic. Since upper Paleolithic times people have gathered round the fire to do just this. A study shows that even deer digest their food less efficiently when eating alone than when eating in packs. When one is forced to eat alone, as at fast-food franchises, the names create an illusion of celebrity or royal companionship—Burger King, Dairy Queen, Roy Rogers."

Society entertainments invariably convert basic primitive needs into symbolic status enhancers. At a society dinner the food often represents affluence and tortured ingenuity. One prominent society hostess admitted as much when she confided that she eats before attending these events so she will not be controlled by her appetite. Preparation time and innovation become central to the formula. At charity benefits we encounter such big-buck displays and/or time-consuming items as caviar, carved ice sculpture, spun-sugar nests for sorbet, and a multitude of culinary choices, from Tex-Mex, sent up from the real Texas, to hundreds of miniature pumpkins filled with pomegranate-seed soup.

today some hostesses struggle to provide party vittles that are neither fattening nor otherwise dangerous, but this effort seldom succeeds. Case in point: Some time ago at a charity dinner hosted by food critic Gael Greene, at a fashionable New York restaurant, out came the new "spa soup" guaranteed to contain no cream, no butter, no animal fat, no sugar. "Then what binds it?" Greene inquired. The waiter trotted off to ask the chef and returned to announce, "Egg yolks."

Rousseau noted, "The savage lives within himself, while social man lives constantly outside himself, so that he seems to receive the consciousness of his own existence merely from the judgment of others concerning him." After the Vanderbilt ball of 1883, American society women raced to outdo one another in seeking such approval. Guests were ushered into lavish ballrooms to view tableaux vivants. After a century of quiescence this display was revived by a hostess in the 1980s at her husband's fiftieth birthday party, although it seems unlikely that in the Gilded Age— as it happened that night—there was a tableau of Rembrandt's Jupiter spying on a real nude or that a male guest climbed right into this Old Master to ogle the naked Danae?

As the last decade of the 1800s wore on, the entertainment became more outré and the boredom escalated. Mrs. Stuyvesant Fish asked guests to a dinner in honor of a Corsican prince with an impeccable pedigree. The prince turned out to be a monkey dressed in white tie and tails. "Here we are again, newer clothes and older faces," Mrs. Fish remarked. Her Jerry Zipkin was a chap named Henry Lehr, who planned a famous dinner on horseback at Louis Sherry's (picture on page 8) and a "dog dinner" at which both his friends and their dogs dined on pâté.

All That and Heaven Too?

This nonsense continued while money tumbled into the pockets of stock inflating, market-manipulating magnificos, and perhaps the rest of the world would not have cared had the optimism and excessive affluence, similar to that of the Reagan eighties, continued. But the bubble burst, followed by hard times and abject poverty. In this climate, excesses like the Bradley Martin ball of 1897 came to be regarded as heinous self-indulgences that would call down the wrath of the gods and the fury of the oppressed.

The problem, then as now, was how to justify this fun. Enter charity, the pure bride that would excuse and validate these forms of entertainment and alleviate the burden of a guilty conscience. The first charitable gesture seemed modest: In 1901, Mary Harriman, the daughter of railroad tycoon E. H. Harriman, proposed that debutantes of her year donate their flowers to city hospitals. She then organized a group of eighty of her compatriots to stage tableaux vivants, the proceeds of which were to go to charity. Thus the Junior League was born, an organization that finally numbered 140 chapters across the United States. All, save the New York League, required community service of their members. Or as one nursemaid explained to another, "The Junior League is that organization that takes care of our children while we're taking care of theirs."

Today the marriage of Charity and Society proceeds apace. The power of the press has escalated as Americans' appetite for image over reality grows to Pantagruelian proportions. More than ever before, reporters create these events in the minds of the public. Few among us are immune. Once upon reading an account of a charity benefit, I turned to my companion and said, "This sounds so glamorous, I wish I'd been there." He replied, "You were."

Celebrities who create the illusion of glamor, power, talent, and heroism have superseded society figures as the main draw at charity benefits, which are seemingly open to anyone with the money for a ticket. This too, of course, is an illusion. As we rely increasingly upon image, the search for validation through identification with the exalted grows more intense than ever. No matter how far away one may be seated, to gaze across the room at a celebrity is to have had dinner with the likes of Barbara Walters, Warren Beatty, Elizabeth Taylor, Tina Turner, Madonna. I sat in the same room as Madonna, therefore I am.

The power of exclusion, even at public events, is still formidable. At a benefit in Aspen organized by Don Henley ostensibly to save Walden Pond (few knew what or where Walden Pond was, or that except for the pond itself little was left of Thoreau's retreat) on a klieg-lighted mall, hundreds jostled one another to plunk down $500 to enter a nightclub where they could rub elbows with Goldie Hawn,

Don Johnson, Melanie Griffith, and Arnold Schwarzenegger—only to find that indeed those celebrities were there but in an inaccessible, roped-off, guarded area.

Some charity benefits have predictable themes—Wild West hoedowns, black and white balls—but what is one to make of a banquet to benefit Oxfam America, an organization dealing with world hunger? At the "Hollywood Hunger Banquet," as it was called, were such celebrities as Mel Gibson, Dustin Hoffman, David Byrne, Taj Mahal, Holly Hunter, and Archbishop Desmond S. Tutu. Guests drew lots to determine where they would sit and what they would eat. According to the *New York Times*, the caterer said, "About seventy-five people will be served by waiters, have a three-course meal, stuffed breast of chicken, sun-dried tomatoes and radicchio salad with shrimp, and a wonderful dessert and wine. . . . The middle percentage will sit on benches at wooden tables. They'll have paper plates with rice and beans and tortillas. And the rest, the majority, will sit on the floor on a mat and have rice and water. . . . Just like the majority of people in the world." The previous year's banquet had included as guests twenty children from Cambodia and El Salvador who had experienced the horrors of war. Said a spokesperson, "These kids lived through the most incredible experiences so they were seated at the 'elite table' because they never had a meal like that."

The marriage of Charity and Society has always been strained. At PEN benefits, speakers such as Jules Feiffer and Roger Rosenblatt have been drowned out by the din of unceasing conversation. And the conceit that a writer would make a desirable host at the table of a $10 thousand patron went awry when Lyndon Johnson's biographer Robert Caro at the end of the evening heard a guest announce that they had been honored by the presence of real estate developer Robert Campeau.

In the process of ratifying our egos and justifying our psychic needs, we drink too much donated wine and eat enough peach melba or chocolate soufflé to put one in a sugar arrest. And we recall that part of the proceeds go to a good cause because once in awhile a disabled child, an ex-drug addict, or political dissident is trotted out to make an appearance (usually just brief enough to make one feel worthy but not to spoil the fun). Yet there is little doubt that this symbiotic, peculiarly American marriage, in posh times or poor, will long endure.

All That and Heaven Too?

d inner

at the

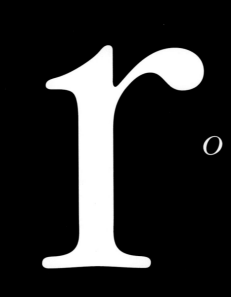

r ound

table

by
*Brendan
Gill*

$\mathcal{D}$inner at the Round Table

Menu

Hors d'Oeuvres
Bacon-Cheese Straws
Crudités
Toasted Nuts
Chorizo-Stuffed Dates

Appetizers
Cheese Biscuits
Tiny Crab Cakes

Entrée
Pot Roast with Double Rich Gravy
Potatoes, Baby Carrots, Pearl Onions
Haricots Verts

Dessert

Apple Cobbler with Vanilla Ice Cream

Saint Véran, 1989

Château Bouscaut, 1970

Hostesses:

Sonny Sloan

and

Geraldine

Stutz

Menu created by Gene Hovis with the generous support of
Macy's Cellar

Brendan Gill, author and longtime drama critic for the New Yorker *reports on being a guest at a Tables of Content dinner given by Sonny Sloan.*

new York City dinner parties bear a close resemblance to theatrical events and are bound to be judged accordingly. Once the usual politeness of farewells has been exchanged ("Good night, good night! Such a lovely evening!" "So glad that you could come!"), the departing guest is transformed into a critic with unexpectedly severe professional standards. Has the party proved to be good theatre or bad? Did the performers enact their roles superbly? Adequately? With or without conviction? In certain unfortunate cases, did the performers appear to have forgotten their lines? If so, were they perhaps understudies—family members pressed into service because some long-counted-upon luminary has come down with the flu? To our sorrow we know that such things happen. No matter! One doesn't give up the theatre of dining out because of them.

The similarity between dinners and dramas is especially evident at the parties that The New York Public Library sponsors annually under the punning rubric Tables of Content. An element of suspense—a certain spice of the unknown—enters into the arrangements for these affairs: Many of the guests are strangers to one another, as well as to the host and hostess, who must gallantly stoop to identifying themselves in their own homes. The start of the evening is uncannily like a curtain going up. One feels a welcome shiver of anticipation, mingled with a prudently suppressed unease: What will the setting be like? The costumes? Most important of all, what is the nature of the plot that is about to unfold? Are we to enjoy a comedy (dear Lord, we hope so) or a tragedy (oh, God, we hope not)?

every Tables of Content dinner is supposed to have a theme, culinary, historical, or what you will. Bound to be more than ordinarily theatrical is a dinner at which the theme chosen calls for actors to read from a designated text. This was to be the highlight of the dinner that Mrs. Irvil Sloan, universally known as "Sonny," would be giving at her Park Avenue apartment on the appointed Tables day. With the insouciant vagueness that so often characterizes Library occasions, I was informed first that the theme would have to do with wit in the 1920s, as manifested at the Algonquin Round Table, and then that it would have to do more specifically with Robert Benchley and Dorothy Parker, as the leading humorists of that celebrated group. I had been one of Benchley's successors in the post of Broadway drama critic of the *New Yorker*. I had also written a short biography of Mrs. Parker and, like her, was a failed Broadway playwright (to fail on Broadway is no disgrace—on the contrary, it is regarded as a kind of success). For these reasons, I was thought to be an appropriate guest at Sonny's dinner, and I accepted an invitation to it with the greatest of pleasure.

Putting on my invisible critic's hat (not so dusty from disuse as I had feared), I took care to be among the first to arrive at her apartment. Long before the first lines of our dinner drama were being spoken upstairs, I took part in a brief, humiliating overture in the ground-floor lobby.

I: "Mrs. Sloan?"

Doorman: "Fifteenth floor, sir."

I: "Thank you. Which apartment on the fifteenth floor?"

Doorman (with a look of ill-disguised contempt): "*All* of the fifteenth floor, sir."

With a rueful shake of the head to indicate that my gaffe had been a mere unthinking slip of the tongue, I stepped into the paneled elevator and was carried upward at a genteel Park Avenue pace to the Sloan apartment. The elevator door opened onto an unattended vestibule. Incense was burning on a side table. Fleetingly, I thought of Dr. Fu Manchu and his hideaway under the streets of London. Nearby was an umbrella stand, chock-a-block with canes and umbrellas, and they, too, struck an English note: that of a velvety green countryside in a mist of rain. I uttered a tentative hello. No answer. Advancing into a big open hall, I called out again, more loudly, "Hello? Hello? Am I in the right place?"

All of a sudden another English note was struck: A large gray and white bearded collie came bounding into the hall to salute me. As it happens, I have little to say to dogs, or they to me. Nevertheless, it is a singular fact of life that dogs woo those who wish to go unwooed; I eyed the sheepdog sternly, hoping to cool its Saxon ardor. At that moment, Sonny Sloan—small, pretty, pert, and wearing fashionable evening slacks—entered the hall, greeted me, and led me by the hand into a cozy dark-walled study, where Elaine Stritch and George Grizzard, the two official stars of the evening, were already seated at their ease, amiably talking shop. Miss Stritch is a tall woman with a cloud of white hair, big eyes, and a breezy manner, no less authentic for serving also, one suspects, as a convenient professional mask. Grizzard—short, gray-haired, and square-jawed, as his name curiously manages to imply—is a skilled teller of stories against himself. In mock despair, he complained to Stritch, Sonny, and me that he had just been offered the role of Polonius in a forthcoming production of *Hamlet*. "When I was young," he said, "I played the prince himself. Not long ago I advanced to Claudius, but I didn't suppose anyone thought I was old enough to play Polonius *yet*. Pol-on-i-us! I take it hard."

Drinks and hors d'oeuvres were served by a smiling waitress, and more guests arrived. Among them was a chunky, dark-haired man named Peter Feibleman, author of a best-selling biography of Lillian Hellman. In the course of conversation, I learned that Feibleman had finished the first draft of a play based on his Hellman biography. Stritch is to star in the play, which, if all goes well, will open in Seattle in the spring and then make its way eastward until it reaches Broadway. Feibleman mentioned that he would like the play to open at the Booth Theatre, where, many years ago, his only other play, *Tyger, Tyger, Burning Bright*, enjoyed a run of several months. Theatre people are a superstitious lot; they seek favorable omens, which are always in short supply. "I'm sure the Booth would bring us good luck," Feibleman says, and Stritch and Grizzard are quick to nod agreement.

By this time, many other guests have arrived and Sonny proposes that we carry our drinks into the drawing room, which is on a scale ample enough to contain without fear of collision fifteen or twenty milling couples of all ages, from the middle twenties (a woman who practices criminal law) to the late eighties (a surgeon who tells me that he has gone from cutting up people to cutting down trees—a judicious change of career). The drawing room occupies a corner of the building; terraces with small trees extend beyond its windows, and out beyond the terraces the million lights of the city blaze against an inky darkness. Some of the guests are strangers to me; others,

like Robert and John, are old friends. Their professional careers aside, in recent years Robert and John have amused themselves with making over houses in out-of-the-way corners of the world; their latest acquisition is a manor house in the Dordogne, which is said to have four acres of roof, all in bad repair.

I meet a young man who, newly arrived from the South, is bent upon making a name for himself as a play director in New York. It turns out that we have a friend in common, the playwright John Guare. I am not surprised to learn that Guare has offered assistance to this promising newcomer. My guess is that if a dozen guests in the room were polled, we would hear a dozen tales of Guare's inveterate generosity. It is this young Southerner who has put together the selections from Benchley and Parker that Stritch and Grizzard will be reading after dinner. Next, I meet a middle-aged woman in a dazzling frilly red dress, who comes romping into the room in a fashion not unlike that of Sonny's affectionate sheepdog. She explains that the invitation had urged everyone to wear "festive dress." "Nobody has ever asked me to do that," she says, "so here I am, doing my best!" She is an artist who keeps an apartment in Venice, on the *imbarcadero* floor of the Palazzo Barbaro. The palazzo belongs to the ancient Foscari family; it was the Foscari who commissioned Palladio to design for them the villa that has long been known as La Malcontenta, on the Brenta canal. I sketch for the lady in red the events of a weekend that I once spent at La Malcontenta, sleeping (or, rather, not sleeping) high up under its tiled attic roof, prey to tireless legions of mosquitoes. I say that I remember the canal as being filled with bobbing, unsinkable plastic bottles and used medical syringes. "Please!" says the lady in red, clapping her hands to her ears. "I'm looking forward to dinner."

In the candlelit dining room, three or four round tables, the hushed, crisp sound of the unfolding of napkins, the gleam and wink of silver, more smiling waitresses and waiters. I am seated between Stritch and Geraldine Stutz, former head of Bendel's and now an editor at Crown. Gerry Stutz, Sonny's cohostess, is to introduce the Stritch-Grizzard reading and she confesses that she has been drawing as much information as possible from my brief biography of Parker. "You knew her," Gerry says. "What was she like?" I answer truthfully, "What would you expect of a humorist? She was the saddest person in the world." Gerry asks, "And Benchley?" The question gives me an opportunity to contradict myself. "What would you expect of a humorist? He was the funniest person in the world."

From table to table, conversation revolves about predictable topics. At our table, we begin a discussion of the many hard-drinking writers in our era who have died comparatively young (including four of my predecessors as drama critics at the *New Yorker*) versus the abstemious writers who have lived on into old age; the conversation falters when none of us can think of an abstemious writer. The dinner, robust and therefore highly agreeable to Stritch ("I'm a diabetic and I can use a lot of carbohydrates"), consists of crab cakes, a beef ragout with potatoes and string beans, an ice cream and pastry dessert, and coffee. White and red wines are served throughout. Only two people at the table smoke, which they do with guilty looks and manifold apologies. "Word of honor! On my mother's grave! I'm seeing an acupuncturist tomorrow."

At Sonny's bidding, we return to the drawing room, where we settle down in an informal half circle of chairs and couches. Two or three of the younger guests choose to sit cross-legged on the floor, in a posture that would crack the hipbones of several of the more elderly ones. The tree-cutting surgeon is preparing to take a discreet postprandial nap in a comfortable chair near the entrance hall. Between the chair and the vestibule, a beeline; foxy grandpa has long since mastered the art of preparing a quick getaway.

Stritch and Grizzard seat themselves side by side at a table that has been moved to a central point in the drawing room. Stutz introduces them with an aplomb that testifies to her skill (acquired in who knows which of her varied careers) at warming up audiences. Stritch and Grizzard read several selections from Benchley's collected writings, then several from Parker's. The audience behaves splendidly, laughing in all the right places. The likenesses between the two authors, who had been close friends and colleagues, are fascinating to observe; still more fascinating are the unlikenesses, well brought out by Stritch and Grizzard. In both cases, the author's humor is intimately related to gender: As a man, Benchley writes of undergoing certain trifling misadventures, to which he more or less cheerfully accommodates himself. As a woman, Parker not only undergoes misadventures—they cause her pain, and we see that the pain is often self-inflicted. With Benchley, we respond by laughing, and that is quite simply that; the episode is ended. With Parker, if we were not laughing, we might well be crying, and to that kind of episode there can be no end.

The reading concludes to much applause. Sonny invites the group to stay on for drinks and further conversation, but in most cases the invitation is politely declined, and for this unsurprising reason: that we are all caught up in the busy-ness of New York in the first weeks of winter, with the joyous hurlyburly of Christmas nearly upon us. Moreover, it has become a commonplace for New Yorkers to say their farewells far earlier than they used to do in the days of the Stork and El Morocco. Men and women alike are up and out of their houses at daybreak because in the strenuous nineties there is always so much work to be got through, so many urgent missions to accomplish. Still smiling at the end of their evening's labors, the staff gathers to help us into our overcoats. Is anyone missing a plaid scarf? Have we both our gloves? The old surgeon is not to be seen; no doubt he is already abed and dreaming of felled spruces. We gather about our indefatigable hostess. "Ah, Sonny, thank you, what a lovely party! Good night, good night!"

As I ride down in the elevator, I begin the accustomed task of all seasoned New York City partygoers: that of passing judgment on the event. Before the elevator reaches the ground floor, I have reached my verdict. The evening has been excellent theatre. The performers, amateurs and professionals alike, have played their assorted roles with distinction. As far as one can tell, there have been no understudies. We have been in the best of company—Stritch and Grizzard, Benchley and Parker—and we perceive, not for the first time and not for the last, that Wallace Stevens, that wary man, was right to assert that words of the world are the life of the world. The pun in the name of the Library's annual occasion has once again been proven apt (and therefore excusable): We have sat at tables and have been content.

Photographs by Henry Grossman

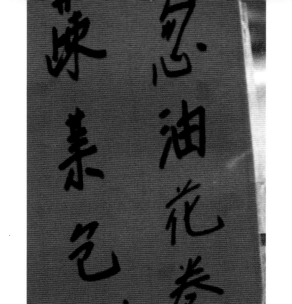

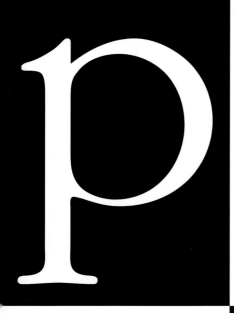

P

retty

decent

C

hinese

takeout

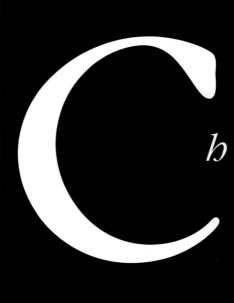

by
Calvin
Trillin

$\mathcal{P}$retty Decent Chinese Takeout

Menu

Dim Sum
Shrimp Dumplings
(The Golden Unicorn)
Stuffed Chinese Eggplant
(The Golden Unicorn)
Leek Dumplings
(The Golden Unicorn)
Fried Tofu Triangles with Flash-Fried
Minced Greens
(The Golden Unicorn)

Cold Course
Cold Seaweed with Garlic (Pell's Dinty)
Sardines (Pell's Dinty)
Cold Lima Beans (Pell's Dinty)
Mock Duck (Hoolok)
Minced Squab Wrapped in Lettuce
Leaves (The Nice Restaurant)
Crispy Rolls with Shrimp and Scallop
(The Nice Restaurant)

Hosts:

Calvin

and Alice

Trillin

Hot Course
Chicken with Lily Flower
(Sun Ko Shing)
Conch with Seafood
(Tai Hong Lau)
Pepper and Salty Shrimp
(Tai Hong Lau)

Dessert
Hong Kong Egg Cakes
(The Woman on Mosco Street)

Tsing-tao beer, 1991

Calvin Trillin, author and food maven, tells what a host must go through—emotionally, gastronomically, intellectually— in order to give a proper Tables of Content dinner.

Y ou might say this started with Chairman Mao. Years ago, I had a fantasy that I had been asked by the State Department to escort Mao Tse-tung on an eating tour of New York. A lot of people thought the fantasy was based on my assumption that Mao had ways of obtaining some of those special dishes that I'm always convinced are being served to Chinese customers in Chinatown and not to me. At the time, frustration over this situation had driven me to carry around a card that said in Mandarin, "Please bring me some of what those people at the next table are having"—a card waiters often handed back to me with a shake of the head and a blunt "You no like." It was assumed that I daydreamed of the Chairman interpreting hitherto mysterious Chinese wall signs in a profoundly perceptive way—don't forget that he was also a poet—or by threatening recalcitrant waiters with fifteen or twenty years in a re-education camp.

In fact, the fantasy wasn't based on Mao's influence in Chinatown but on the assumption that having a busy head of state in tow would give me an excuse to employ a method of dining I had never worked up the nerve to try: one favorite dish at each restaurant. Unless my party included a person of international stature, I had always figured, a restaurant proprietor might get a bit testy if we walked in, sat down, and instructed the waiter, "Just a large plate of those splendid hash browns of yours, please." My fantasy settled on Mao Tse-tung as the person of international stature involved, I think, for no reason beyond the fact that, as my friend Fats Goldberg, the pizza baron, might have put it, Mao looked like a man who liked his groceries.

In my fantasy, though, the tour turns out to be made to order for the Chairman. He loves the constant movement as we eat a plate of soft-clam bellies in Brooklyn, then dash to midtown Manhattan for a salmon-skin handroll. It reminds him of the Long March—although, I discover in dinner-table chitchat, it turns out that almost everything reminds him of the Long March.

e ventually, it dawned on me that takeout food could be gathered up one dish at a time without embarrassment even if the Chairman didn't happen to be along. I'm sure that it would have pleased Mao to know that Chinese takeout was what I had in mind. We happen to live in Greenwich Village, within easy bike or car range of Chinatown. In fact, particularly if we have a guest from out of town,.we like to walk to lunch in Chinatown— strolling through the Village and the Italian South Village and Soho and Little Italy on the way, and then following a dim sum lunch by treating the guest to a game of tic-tac-toe

Pretty Decent Chinese Takeout

Trillin unstintingly dedicated himself to many tasting tours of Chinatown involving lunches and dinners and alfresco samplings on the street to assure that his "pretty decent" Chinese take-out meal would be more than that—that it would, in fact, be terrific. He consulted a restaurateur (top left), carefully considered everything from ducks to dumplings, selected the ultimate chopsticks and the perfect tea, and then carried it all home. Unpacking and organizing (top row, near left) was a logistical operation requiring the managerial skills of both Trillins. Guests began the dinner with Chinese finger food and were then summoned to the table by bullhorn (bottom center), although there were no dawdlers getting to the feast.

against a live chicken at the Chinese Arcade on Mott Street. When we wanted to eat Chinese food at home, we had always fetched takeout from Chinatown rather than order in from one of the neighborhood purveyors of brown glop. But why, I finally realized, should we limit ourselves to a single restaurant for the entire meal? There was nothing discourteous about ordering a single dish to go. Why not collect a favorite dish from a number of restaurants—the way I always imagined doing it with Chairman Mao?

We put our plan into action. To make certain everything would arrive home hot, of course, the operation had to be carefully planned. Two or three people, their watches synchronized and their assignments memorized, would fan out from a waiting car to a number of different restaurants—say, Phoenix Garden, an old Cantonese favorite of ours, for pepper and salty shrimp, and Shanghai Gourmet for cold lima beans, and one of the East Broadway Szechuan joints for sesame noodles—and then rush back to the car for the dash back to our house. Because of the split-second timing and military precision involved, we took to calling it the Entebbe Raid.

The Entebbe Raid had long been our standard procedure for Chinese takeout by 1983, when the New York Public Library held its first Tables of Content dinners— nearly a hundred volunteer hosts throwing dinner parties on the same night to raise money for the Library. The dinners—listed in a fat folder of invitations so that the paying guests could decide which one to sign up for—had titles like A Monticello Memory ("A salute to the great gourmet Thomas Jefferson, with some of the foods he introduced to the United States—and music of the period") and Dinner with Edward VII ("A formal twelve-course dinner featuring the king's favorite dishes").

The Tables of Content evening was a great success, which didn't surprise me. As it happens, the various volunteer committees of the New York Public Library have become tremendously skilled at throwing parties. The reason is simple: Try to imagine building a fund-raising event around somebody arranging to get a book down from the stacks. Unlike some cultural institutions that have natural opportunities to produce the sort of glittering occasions that donors live for—the preview of a huge Impressionist show at the Metropolitan Museum of Art, for instance, or opening night of *Rigoletto* at the Metropolitan Opera—the Library does not in the normal course of its business produce any boffo events. There are not even any functions for which the Library can sell tickets at benefit prices: One of its glories is that nobody has to pay to use its facilities, ever.

To ensure a steady stream of funds, the Library had to become imaginative at providing its own bread and circuses—and the Tables of Content evenings soon became a fixture. Every other year, seventy-five or a hundred New York families would have perhaps a dozen guests, many of them strangers, for a special meal—a fifteenth-century French Christmas banquet, for instance ("Guests will dine on the cuisine of the great chef Taillevant. Menu: Brouet d'Allemagne, porcelet, rosty, gallimaufre de mouton, and venoisin") or an evening devoted to old Vienna ("A six-course dinner celebrating turn-of-the-century Vienna and Secessionist painter Gustav Klimt in the presence of His Excellency the Ambassador of Austria and Mrs. Klestil"). By the time the fourth evening of dinners came around, an evening that included A Raj Banquet at Princely Hyderabad and a dinner called simply Anna Karenina ("Feast on dozens of oysters, relish the turbot, savor the soup, sample the champagne, and revel in the lavish style of pre-Revolutionary Russia as you relive Levin and Oblonsky's splendid dinner at Angleterre in Moscow"), my wife and I began thinking that we should probably get involved as hosts. Naturally, our thoughts turned to Chairman Mao. We offered to have fourteen guests at a dinner called Pretty Decent Chinese Takeout. When I was asked by the Tables of Content committee how our meal should be described on the invitation, I said, "No eating directly from the carton allowed."

m̲y plan was to put on a slightly more elaborate version of the Entebbe Raid—some reheating, table settings that did not call to mind a fraternity house that was about to have its charter revoked, fewer arguments at the table about which street-corner cart in Chinatown had the best scallion pancakes. I got a bit concerned, though, when we received the invitation listing the seventy-nine Tables of Content dinners that would be held the night we were offering Chinese takeout. It had some evenings that sounded stimulating—a dinner that featured two noted architects discussing modern American architecture, for instance, dinners that amounted to evenings spent in the company of noted authors or political figures—and some evenings that sounded like major culinary events. The dinner listed just above ours was called The Three Musketeers Meet D'Artagnan, and its description said: "Journey through time to nineteenth-century southwestern France to meet Alexandre Dumas's legendary musketeers. Guest chef Ariane Daguin will create a Gascon banquet of foie gras and duck specialties with complementary fine wines selected by wine consultant Peter J. Morrell." Would anybody, for the same price—a rather steep price, as it happened—prefer to have pretty decent Chinese takeout? I had assumed we were going a bit beyond the normal Entebbe Raid, but I wasn't sure we were up to the invasion of Normandy.

Then, remembering the Chairman's perseverance on the Long March, I got hold of myself. We might not be able to offer sophisticated atmosphere—I had, after a brief conversation with my wife, abandoned a plan to have as a centerpiece an avant-garde construction made of those little white takeout cartons—but we would make up for it with fantastic food. Some dishes we routinely acquired in an Entebbe Raid would have knocked D'Artagnan off his feet. We knew we had available the Phoenix Garden's pepper and salty shrimp. We had minced squab wrapped in lettuce leaves from The Nice on East Broadway. For dessert, I knew we could serve the Hong Kong egg cakes a woman on Mosco Street makes in a tiny shed—delicacies I had once described as tasting what madeleines would taste like if the French really understood such things.

I was confident we could count on some superior dim sum dumplings as appetizers. At a dim sum meal, of course, you simply point to whatever you want on the carts that are pushed by—in my experience, there is no such thing as a dim sum cart pusher in Chinatown who speaks English—so we didn't actually know the names of our favorites, but we had always managed to make ourselves understood. At the Oriental Pearl on Mott Street above Canal, we were particularly fond of vegetable dumplings that we called, because of their shapes, Hockey Pucks, and even more fond of huge rectangles of slippery rice noodles wrapped loosely around shrimp— a dish that my daughters had always called, with a great deal of respect, Slime. In our family, there has long been a unanimous belief that Slime is irresistible. Thinking

about having such dishes at our disposal cheered me up, until I rode my bike to Chinatown and found the Phoenix Garden's building boarded up, about to be demolished.

What sort of Entebbe Raid has no pepper and salty shrimp?" I asked my wife. "You'd better call Colette," my wife suggested.

Colette Rossant is a friend and neighbor who writes cookbooks and reviews restaurants and cooks so well that, as I've admitted before, when we're invited to dinner at her house my wife has to hold my jacket to prevent me from traveling at a steady, uncharacteristic trot. Colette discovers restaurants as routinely as Indian scouts in Western movies pick up trails, and Chinatown happens to be one of her specialties. The first thing she told me was that rice noodles can't be reheated. Slime was out.

Discouraged? I would have been if Colette and I hadn't arranged to have a strategy session in Chinatown. We met at the Golden Unicorn on East Broadway, which happens to be the sort of restaurant I couldn't have imagined existing in Chinatown when I first began to fantasize about Chairman Mao. For years, the Chi-

Chinese beer was the drink of choice, as the courses kept coming and coming and coming.

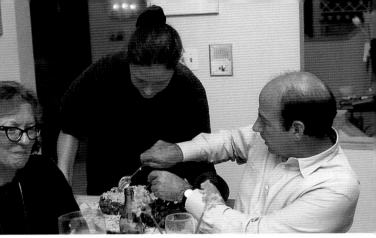

nese restaurants I patronized had been Formica-table places, where you brought your own beer and tried to explain to your visiting cousin from Kansas City, who had secretly wanted to go to Mamma Leone's, that atmosphere wasn't everything. If a restaurant with a beer license or a flashy facade or a credit-card sticker on the window had appeared in Chinatown, I believe I would have treated it as a mirage. But partly because of an influx of immigrants from Hong Kong, many of them prosperous people who wouldn't think of walking into the dumps we treasured, Chinatown now has a number of luxuriously appointed restaurants—including the Golden Unicorn, which many people believe serves the best dim sum in New York.

Colette introduced me to Cindy Wo, the manager, who said we could easily pick up dumplings cold in the morning—in Chinatown restaurants they are strictly for daytime consumption—and then steam them at home. We decided on shrimp dumplings and stuffed Chinese eggplant and some leek dumplings that, I had to admit, tasted at least as good as Hockey Pucks. We also decided we could get some fried tofu triangles with flash-fried minced greens to serve as hors d'oeuvres. After we had tried all of that and some other items that happened to be wheeled past our table while we were involved in the decision-making process ("Well, as long as we're here . . ."), I told Colette that I could feel my confidence returning.

the lunch at the Golden Unicorn was the first of a number of research trips I made to Chinatown. Colette suggested that I try something called "baby pig" at a coffee shop on Mott Street and cold rolled rice noodles at a coffee shop on Division Street. Other denizens of Chinatown I know volunteered suggestions—the mussel casserole with cellophane noodles at the Mandarin Court and the seafood in a taro basket at the Oriental Town Sea Food restaurant and a sort of Chinese ham sandwich that the Canton on Division Street usually calls buns. I felt obligated to taste all of these; the Library, after all, is an institution close to my heart.

At the sort of storefront restaurants that have cold dishes displayed in the window, I tried three versions of cold lima beans—finally settling on the ones at Pell's Dinty, a Shanghainese restaurant on Pell Street that I have always treasured for both its bean curd and its improbably Irish-sounding name. While I was there, I also decided to include some cold seaweed with garlic and, unable to resist, some tiny sardines—about the size of paper matches, just big enough to allow an alert diner to stare into their tiny little eyes. All of those would be part of the cold course, along with a dish from Hoolok on East Broadway, where I am very fond of the mock duck—bean curd shaped in a way that makes it look remarkably like a duck, although not enough like a duck, I think, to fool another duck.

I felt I was getting things in hand. The

Nice would provide the minced squab in lettuce leaves, plus some crispy rolls with shrimp and scallop. With Colette's help, I decided on a couple of hot dishes from Tai Hong Lau on Mott Street—conch with seafood and a credible version of the essential pepper and salty shrimp—and some chicken with lily flower from Sun Ko Shing on East Broadway. To me, I told Colette, the lily flower tasted a bit more like marigold, but I wasn't going to quibble. I checked with the Hong Kong egg cake woman to make sure she would be open at the strategic time. I arranged to borrow a couple of electric steamers from Colette for the reheating operation. I had another conversation with my wife—this one even shorter—about a centerpiece of takeout cartons. We were ready.

We hit Chinatown in a series of Entebbe raids—starting in the late morning, when we picked up the dumplings, and ending in the evening, just before the guests arrived, when we jumped into a cab on Mott Street with boxes full of steaming Chinese food that included sixteen fully stuffed conch shells. "It all seemed to go like clockwork," my second-in-command said to me, as the cab shook loose of the Chinatown traffic and headed toward our house.

"Textbook," I said. "You'd have to call it textbook."

A success! Definitely. The food came out just when it was supposed to, and in the shape it was supposed to be in. The guests seemed to love it. They even ate the tiny sardines—causing me to wonder, just for a moment, whether I made a mistake not trying them out on chicken feet. When dessert came, it was proven, once again, that it is impossible to buy enough Hong Kong egg cakes. All in all, I felt we had done our duty. My only regret—except for the centerpiece—was the title and description of the dinner in the invitation. Upon reflection, I decided that we had been overly restrained. If we ever do it again, I think we'll call our dinner A Banquet with Chairman Mao, and describe it as "a festival of oriental specialties, of the sort nearly enjoyed by Chairman Mao Tse-tung on an eating tour of New York."

Photographs by Martha Holmes

Pretty Decent Chinese Takeout

a

all

that

j azz

*Barbara
Costikyan*

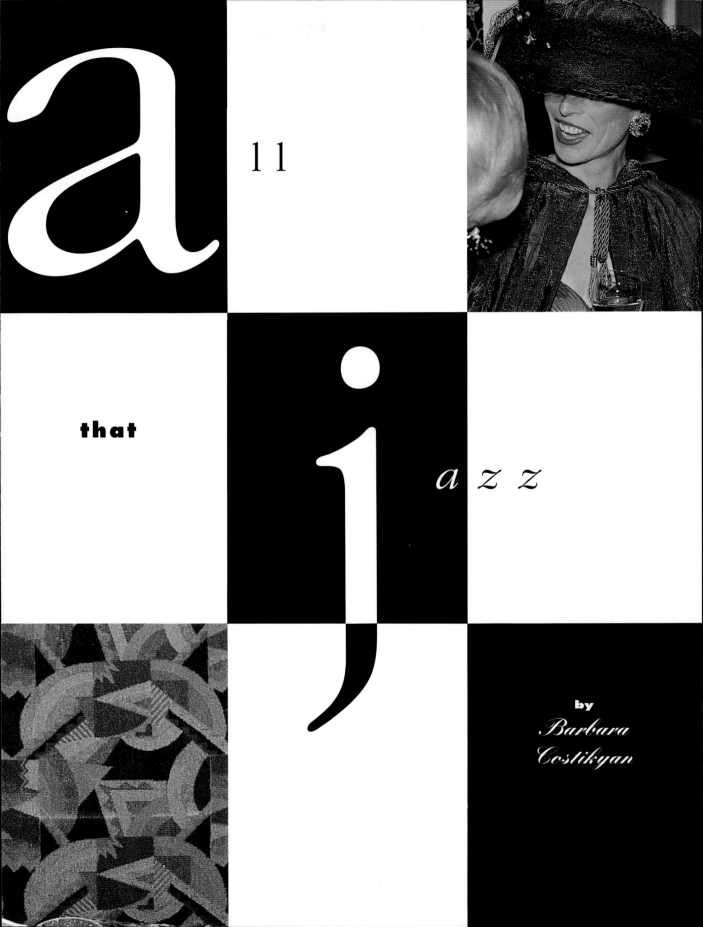

All That Jazz

Menu

Hors d'Oeuvres
Cheese Straws

Baby Crab Cakes

Cheddar Corn Muffins with Country Ham

Crudités with Herb Mayonnaise

Assorted Olives

Appetizer
Baby Lettuce with Citrus Vinaigrette

Entrée
Chef Eileen Weinberg's
Seafood Jambalaya with Scallops,
Jumbo Shrimp, Tasso, and Andouille*

Stewed Okra and Tomatoes

Roasted Leeks

Parsley Buttermilk Biscuits

Dessert
Pecan Pie

Macedoine of Fruit

Romanée-Conti, 1974

Chef: Eileen Weinberg

Hosts:

Barbara and Ed Costikyan,

Susan and David Kraus,

Isobel and Ronald Konecky

*An asterisk denotes that the recipe for the dish is included.

On the second floor of Ron and Isobel Konecky's East Side brownstone, twenty-four jazz lovers were listening to pianist Billy Taylor reminisce about the Manhattan music scene of the 40s and 50s. He was seated at an upright piano near an old mahogany bar, but his audience relaxed in chairs, on sofas, the stairway, and the floor. They had drinks in their hands and smiles on their faces. The cohosts were Barbara and Ed Costikyan and Susan and David Kraus.

Billy Taylor recalled how as a young musician he had used the jazz archives of the Library's Schomburg Center for Research in Black Culture and that he was forever grateful. "Most nights," he said, "I would play with Charlie Parker or Dizzy Gillespie at Minton's Playhouse." He spoke about Eubie Blake. "Eubie lived for one hundred years and seven days and was a consummate teacher. He told me to use my left hand more." Then Mr. Taylor played an improvisation of "All the Things You Are" with his left hand. Most of the guests hadn't even been born when jazz came to Harlem in the 1920s, but some were teenagers in the 40s and 50s and had grown up on the sounds of swing, boogie, and gospel that Mr. Taylor was playing.

Downstairs in the kitchen, Chef Eileen Weinberg, owner of Good & Plenty, a gourmet and catering store, was preparing jambalaya. Jambalaya, she said, was a dish made for Taylor's music but not for the Koneckys' narrow stove. When she had seen the house weeks earlier, she told Isobel Konecky, "I need another oven." Friends Betty and Bernie Jacobs, who live in the next-door building, agreed to lend their kitchen and to be away from their house the night of the dinner.

At 8:30 when the jazz concert was over, the hosts, the guests, and the pianist went downstairs to the dining room for a seated dinner. Nobody thought to glance out the windows onto the dark street where Chef Weinberg and her white-uniformed staff were shuttling back and forth between buildings, lugging huge pots of seafood and rice. Instead, everybody was watching host Ron Konecky hold and pour a Methuselah of 1974 Romanée-Conti.

Photographs by John Chew

Quimper and candles set the mood for a festive informal dinner. The antique French country china

seems just right for a Creole-inspired dinner accompanied by a magnificent French wine.

Chef Eileen Weinberg's Seafood Jambalaya with Scallops, Jumbo Shrimp, Tasso, and Andouille

✳

1 pound sweet butter
3 large onions, diced
1 head celery, diced
3 tablespoons chopped garlic cloves
3 large yellow bell peppers, diced
3 large red bell peppers, diced
1½ pounds tasso (spicy Creole ham), diced
12 andouille sausages, sliced
4 red chilies
4 pounds tomatoes, diced
6 jalapeño peppers, chopped or sliced
6 bay leaves
3 or 4 branches lemon thyme
6 cups long-grain rice
8 cups boiling chicken stock
4 tablespoons hot sauce
5 pounds jumbo prawns, peeled and deveined
8 pounds sea scallops

1. Preheat the oven to 350°F. Melt the butter in a 10- to 12-quart pot. Sauté the onions, celery, and garlic until the onions are translucent.

2. Add the yellow and red peppers, tasso, and andouille, and cook for about 10 minutes. Add the chilies, tomatoes, jalapeños, bay leaves, and thyme, and cook an additional 5 to 10 minutes. Add the rice and cook, stirring occasionally, for 5 to 10 minutes, until the rice is well coated with the ingredients. Add the boiling chicken stock and 2 tablespoons hot sauce. Stir very well and taste the stock for seasoning. Add the additional 2 tablespoons hot sauce if desired. (The andouille and the tasso can be very spicy. The hot sauce can be omitted if you wish.)

3. Stir in the prawns and scallops, cover, and bake for approximately 45 minutes to an hour. Cooking times vary depending on how much the rice has cooked before it goes into the oven, so check the rice from time to time during baking.

Serves 25

Opening—and sampling—the Romanée Conti is serious business for cohost Ron Konecky (above). Cohostess Barbara Costikyan, (opposite page, top picture, standing), a noted food writer, talks with her guests, including guest of honor pianist Billy Taylor, seated left. The chefs of the evening, led by Eileen Weinberg (bottom picture) take a well-deserved bow.

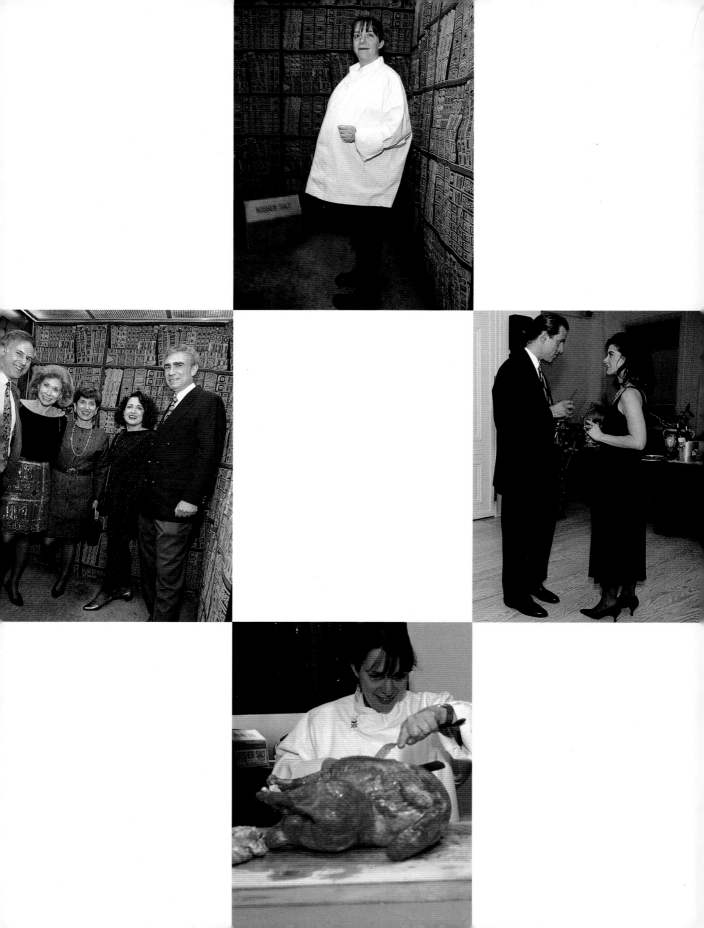

a

l

iterary

feast

by

*Eleanor
Graves*

A Literary Feast

Menu

From Babette's Feast
by Isak Dinesen
Mock Turtle Soup
Blinis Demidoff*

From Portrait of the Artist as a
Young Man *by James Joyce*
Turkey
Winter Root Vegetables

From To the Lighthouse
by Virginia Woolf
Boeuf en Daube

From Swann's Way
by Marcel Proust
Madeleines
A Literary Cake

Amontillado Sherry
Assorted Wines

Chef: Anne Rosenzweig

*An asterisk denotes that the recipe for the dish is included.

Hosts:

Joan Vass,

Peter Duchin,

and Brooke

Hayward

When the Library separately asked author Brooke Hayward, designer Joan Vass, and band leader Peter Duchin to give a Tables of Content dinner, the two longtime friends and neighbors thought it would be the most natural thing—as well as the most fun—to team up and do a party together. They decided at once that, in an obvious homage to the Library, it should be a literary feast, and since they both live in the same Manhattan building, that it should be a movable one as well.

"It was Joan's conceit that we should have food from twentieth-century novels," says Brooke Hayward. "This limitation made everything much harder, since in the nineteenth-century people *really* ate. In fact, it became a *travail*, but we did it anyway."

"I read these books in my youth," says Joan. "Joyce is my favorite twentieth-century writer, and I had just reread a wonderful description of a Christmas turkey in *Portrait of the Artist*. That really gave me the idea."

Brooke came up with *Babette's Feast* by Isak Dinesen with its wonderful descriptions of food—although the story does not eulogize food the way the movie did, as the two women found out after a rereading.

The *boeuf en daube* from Virginia Woolf's *To the Lighthouse* was Joan's inspiration. The immortal madeleines from *Swann's Way* was an obvious must to them both.

"Joan wanted to do the wedding cake from *Goodbye, Columbus*, but I drew the line at a wedding cake."

But Joan would not settle without a cake. She decided on a cake resembling a stack of all the books that inspired the party, with Joyce's *Portrait of the Artist* on the top of the stack, open to the very first line of the very first page, "Once upon a time . . . " "When I thought of that, I cried," she says.

Master cake baker Sylvia Weinstock was called upon to turn this literary tour de force into a culinary triumph, which was duly accomplished in a flurry of sugar and chocolate and frostings of many colors. The result was an edible trompe l'oeil.

Chef Anne Rosenzweig, the genius of New York's Arcadia restaurant, created the rest of the menu, starting with Blinis Demidoff and Mock Turtle Soup, both from *Babette's Feast*. "The turtle soup in *Feast* was the real thing, but we would never have killed a real turtle," says Joan.

As guests arrived at Brooke's apartment, they were met with music by Brooke's husband, pianist and orchestra leader Peter Duchin, and by Brooke wearing a black and white pajama outfit by, of course, Joan Vass. Although the guests could have anything they wanted to drink, they were encouraged to have Amontillado sherry, the drink of choice in *Babette's Feast*. Playwright John Guare read the appropriate section of Dinesen's work. After cocktails, appetizers, and soup, it was off to Joan's apartment, via an elevator hung with

a trompe l'oeil fabric that looked like bookshelves.

At Joan's a laden buffet table awaited. The turkey, the beef, a giant platter of glazed vegetables, and finally the incredible edible cake. More readings, more wine. Everyone left feeling not only that they had been gloriously well fed, but that after this evening they were delightfully well read. Literary and luscious—what Library could ask for more?

Photographs by Arlene Gottfreid

The hosts—writer Brooke Hayward;
her husband, orchestra leader Peter
Duchin (lower far left); and designer
Joan Vass (lower left)—greet guests in
both their apartments, which are one
floor apart. There were readings by
playwright John Guare to enjoy (upper
left), after which John Guare himself
(above) enjoyed the buffet.

A Literary Feast

Blinis Demidoff

✳

1½ cups corn kernels, preferably fresh
½ cup milk
⅓ cup cornmeal
⅓ cup flour
4 tablespoons sweet butter, melted
2 eggs
2 egg yolks
½ teaspoon salt
½ teaspoon pepper
¼ cup chopped fresh chives
½ cup clarified sweet butter
Crème Fraîche (recipe follows)
Assorted caviars (osetra, sevruga, golden
    whitefish, salmon roe, or the like—as much
    as your budget will allow)

1. Roughly chop the corn kernels, or process in short pulses in a food processor, until a chunky but creamy consistency is reached.

2. Place the corn kernels in a large bowl and whisk in the milk, cornmeal, and flour, making sure there are no lumps.

3. In a separate bowl, whisk together the melted butter, whole eggs, and egg yolks. Stir into the corn mixture and season with the salt, pepper, and half the chives.

4. To a large sauté pan over medium-high heat add all the clarified butter. Pour in the batter to make pancakes the size of silver dollars. Cook for 2 minutes, or until golden brown on one side, then flip. Cook for 2 more minutes. Remove from the pan using a slotted spatula; place 4 cooked corn cakes on each serving plate. Repeat the process until all the batter is used.

5. Garnish each serving with a large dollop of crème fraîche and assorted caviars. Sprinkle with the remaining chives.

Serves 6

Crème Fraîche

✳

Prepare 2 days in advance.

2 cups heavy cream
3 tablespoons buttermilk

1. At least 2 days in advance, combine the cream and buttermilk in a glass or ceramic container. Cover with plastic wrap and place in a warm area for approximately 24 hours.

2. When the cream has thickened, place the container in the refrigerator for at least 24 hours.

After playing the piano, Peter admires a guest who performs.

Guests wander through the two apartments and settle wherever they choose.

Anne Rosenzweig, the acclaimed chef of Arcadia restaurant, is a hands-on cook.

At the end of the evening, John Guare takes a bow with his hostess Brooke.

the

he

m oderns

by

*Jacqueline
Weld*

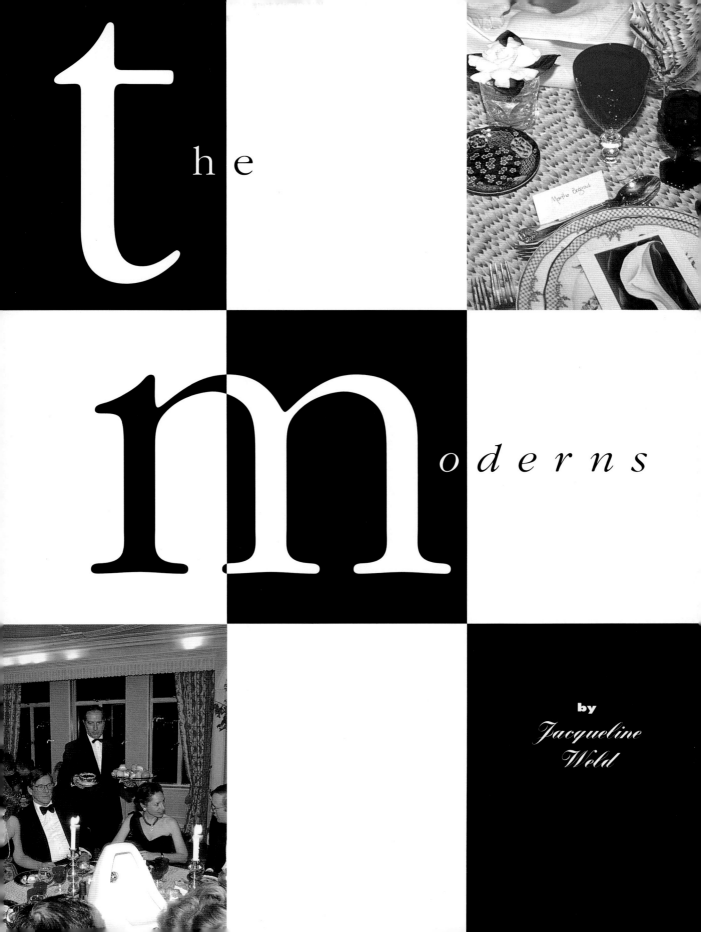

The Moderns

Menu

Appetizer
Spicy Shrimp Georgia O'Keeffe with
Grilled Vegetables

Entrée
Chocolate Chicken à la Peggy
Guggenheim via André Breton*
Green Rice Magritte
Madcap Salad à la Duchamp

Dessert
Profiteroles Man Ray

Assorted Wines

*An asterisk denotes that the recipe for the dish is included.

Hosts:

Jacqueline and

Matthew Weld,

Roxana and

Hamilton

Robinson

roxana Robinson and I decided it would be fun to work—or rather play—together. I had given a Library dinner before—a Surrealist party—and thought it would improve matters to have a cohost. We decided it should be a biographer's dinner since we had both written biographies of twentieth-century art figures: Georgia O'Keeffe in Roxana's case, Peggy Guggenheim in mine. We invited Calvin Tomkins as a guest since he was at work on a biography of Marcel Duchamp.

We had an O'Keeffe dinner table centered by a huge bleached steer's skull rented from Maxilla and Mandible, a West Side shop that sells only bones. We put the skull on a crisp white linen napkin and surrounded it with votive candles. Calla lily menu cards competed with the real white calla lilies from Anthony's that we had strewn about the house.

At the Guggenheim dinner table we had a signed R. Mutt urinal, a homage to our guest Calvin Tomkins. This still managed to shock a few guests and waiters, so many years after Duchamp entered one at the Society of Independent Artists as his breathlessly awaited sequel to *Nude Descending a Staircase*. Red long-stemmed roses crisscrossed the urinal.

Scattered around the house were antlers brought by Roxana and more bones. We replaced ordinary photographs with surreal images in the picture frames, making my "family" look mighty odd indeed.

We tried to invent dishes that the moderns might have served. We began with spicy shrimp and grilled vegetables. As concocted by the Silver Palate, it blended the Western-style spices with the simple vegetables that were O'Keeffe's favorites. We followed that with Chocolate Chicken, a recipe André Breton brought back from Mexico after paying an adulatory visit to Leon Trotsky. Peggy Guggenheim loved serving this Aztec Chocolate Chicken to guests at her palazzo on the Grand Canal. We teamed the chicken with a bright emerald green rice Magritte and a madcap salad à la Duchamp, who was a master of the very odd mix.

Most of the fun came from inventing ourselves. We had asked the guests to come as a painting from the period or, for the less adventurous, in black tie. Roxana dressed head to toe in black, with white collar and cuffs, and a broad-brimmed black O'Keeffe hat. I came perversely as one of Matisse's odalisques because Peggy had never bought a Matisse—he wasn't abstract enough to suit her. Our husbands, Tony Robinson and Matt Weld, opted for the simpler black tie. So did Calvin Tomkins, but Roxana made him put on another O'Keeffe hat. One of our guests arrived as Peggy Guggenheim herself, with outrageous sunglasses and a costume reminiscent of the severe black-and-gold Ken Scott sheath Peggy liked to pose in.

We all had a marvelous time planning the party and greeting our guests, all of

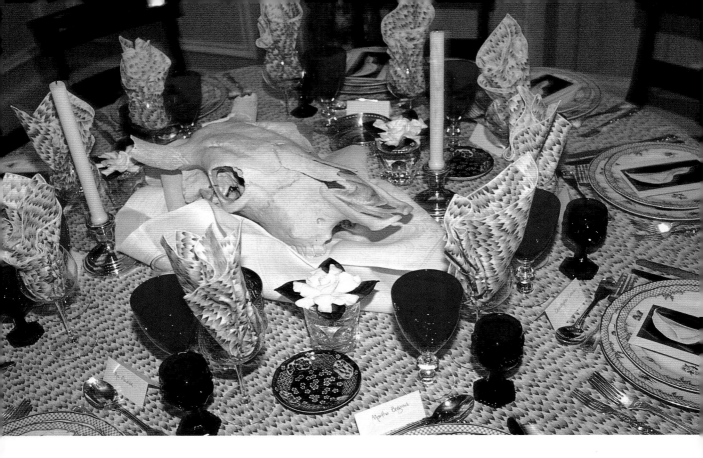

whom had an interest in the arts. Next day we returned the skull and bones to Maxilla and Mandible.

Photographs by James McGoon

Chocolate Chicken à la Peggy Guggenheim via André Breton

✳

If you want Aztec authenticity, you should consider a paste of hot chilies (6 dried ancho, or 4 dried mulato, or 4 dried pasilla, which you will pull the stems off, run under cold water, break, crush or pulverize, remove the seeds from, and soak in boiling water for 30 minutes) and ¾ cup almonds, which you will grind together with the combustibles.

I, however, prefer it inauthentic and much milder without the chilies.

2 chickens (about 2½ to 3 pounds each), which you have slapped about a little bit and cut into eighths
Oil for browning
2 medium onions, chopped up and made to cry
2 celery stalks, rigidly chopped up
2 garlic cloves, minced and winced
1 large (32-ounce) can plum tomatoes, opened with a nail file

1 can chicken broth with the serrated edges

The following spices of life: 2 tablespoons
    sesame seeds, ½ teaspoon coriander, ½
    teaspoon cinnamon, and salt and pepper

If you like them (I don't use): ½ teaspoon
    ground cloves and ½ teaspoon anise seeds

½ cup raisins

4 cubes unsweetened chocolate, preferably
    disagreeable

1 delicious Hershey bar

1. In a large casserole, over medium flame, brown the chicken pieces in oil until delightfully golden but not cooked, and reserve.

2. In the same oil, toss in with abandon the onions, the celery stalks, and the unhappy garlic cloves until they, too, beg, wilting, for mercy. And then return the chicken and add the tomatoes, chicken broth, and spices. If you are using the chili and almond paste, add it to the pot now.

3. Throw in the raisins and the chocolates—delicious and sour.

4. Cover and cook for about 30 minutes, until the whole burbles up and grabs you and you like the way it tastes, adding Hershey bars or nuts or whatever you want so that when you are asked for the recipe it will be an impossibility to re-create.

Serves 6 to 8

A steer's skull makes a
striking centerpiece (opposite) and is
an homage to Georgia O'Keeffe.
Above, hostesses Jackie Weld and
Roxanna Hamilton dressed
for the arty occasion—Jackie as a
Matisse odalisque, Roxanna as
O'Keeffe herself; guest of honor author
Calvin Tomkins obligingly sports
an O'Keeffe-style hat.

a n

e ducated

palate

by
Hannah
Pakula

POUDRE DE PERLES

An Educated Palate

Menu

Hors d'Oeuvres
Assorted Crudités
Cheese Puffs

Appetizer
Smoked Salmon Garnished with
New Potatoes Stuffed with Caviar
and Caper Berries

Entrée
Crown Roast of Lamb Stuffed
with Lamb and Rice
Mixed Steamed Baby Vegetables
Field Greens Salad with Vinaigrette

Dessert
Crème Brûlée*

Monterey Chardonnay,
Limited Release, 1988
Château Gruaud-Larose, 1985
Perrier-Jouët Brut

Hosts:

Elizabeth and

Felix Rohatyn,

Hannah and Alan

Pakula

*An asterisk denotes that the recipe for the dish is included.

eighteen people gathered to meet Joseph Fernanadez, then New York City School Chancellor, at a dinner given by Elizabeth and Felix Rohatyn and Hannah and Alan Pakula at the Pakulas' apartment. They were seated at two tables and ate Scotch salmon, crown roast of lamb, and crème brûlée.

To start the discussion, Elizabeth Rohatyn asked each of the guests what he or she would wish for education in our city, given the power to wave a magic wand. The wish list was varied, including such things as citywide early educational programs to prepare children before kindergarten, literacy for both parents and children, an increase in interactive computer learning, and the presence of one or even two concerned parents in the home to back up the educational process.

Chancellor Fernandez brought the discussion back to earth. He reminded the guests that 60 percent of the students in New York City schools are drawn from single-parent households. "The odds they are facing are very, very dramatic," he said. Both Chancellor Fernandez and Dr. Patricia Ewers, president of Pace University and one of the guests, noted that schools have in effect become full-service social agencies, providing meals, health care, and the kind of basic support once found in the home. "We are part of the infrastructure of the city," Fernandez noted, "but we don't have our fair share of the resources."

The chancellor said that schools are still recovering from the budget squeeze of the mid-1970s and that many lack such basic facilities as libraries and even rudimentary art and music programs. He noted that the school system had taken a $430,000,000 total cut in state and city funding this year. "We've run out of ideas and gimmicks," he said.

Chancellor Fernandez concluded that it was time to wake up the federal government and implement a Marshall Plan for the schools. He pointed to a lack of governmental leadership, noting that when the United States faced a similar challenge over *Sputnik* and the space program some years ago, Americans were able to find the commitment and resources necessary not only to compete with but to surpass our competition.

Photographs by Sally Phipps

Crème Brûlée

✳

This recipe comes from the old (1961) *New York Times Cookbook,* edited by Craig Claiborne. I used it for years, until our sugar became so processed that it would no longer melt over the custard. I mentioned this recently to Anne Isaak of Elio's Restaurant. Anne went into their kitchen and produced a box of Whitworth's Demerara Cane Sugar from England. It melts like the old stuff. I am happy. Apparently, the guests were too.

I prepare the custard the day before serving, chill it overnight, and melt the sugar the next morning, returning it to the refrigerator until serving time.

3 cups heavy cream
6 tablespoons sugar, plus sugar for topping
6 egg yolks
2 teaspoons (or more) vanilla extract

1. Preheat the oven to 300°F.

2. Heat the cream in a double boiler until it is very hot, and stir in the sugar.

3. Beat the egg yolks until very pale. (I use an electric mixer.) When the yolks are light enough, reduce the mixer speed and add the hot cream gradually.

4. When the custard is mixed, add the vanilla (the original recipe calls for 2 teaspoons, but I always put in a little extra).

5. Strain through a sieve into a straight-sided baking dish. Put the dish into a pan containing about an inch of boiling-hot water (this is a bain-marie). It should bake for around an hour and a half. (The original recipe says 35 minutes; the least I've ever cooked it in is 65 minutes, and it usually takes more time.) The custard is done when a knife blade inserted near the edge comes out clean, nearly clean in the center. Another test is to shake it gently. It should be fairly firm.

6. Chill.

7. The next day, cover the chilled custard with an even layer of sugar. Place the baking dish in a pan and surround it with ice cubes. Heat under the broiler until the sugar melts. Watch very carefully to be sure it doesn't burn. Chill again until time to serve.

Serves 6 to 8

Recipe by Hannah Pakula

*Joseph Fernandez is
flanked by his hostesses
Hannah Pakula,
left, and Elizabeth
Rohatyn, right.*

*Dinner conversation was lively and continued well into the evening. When Felix Rohatyn
makes a point, guests listen.*

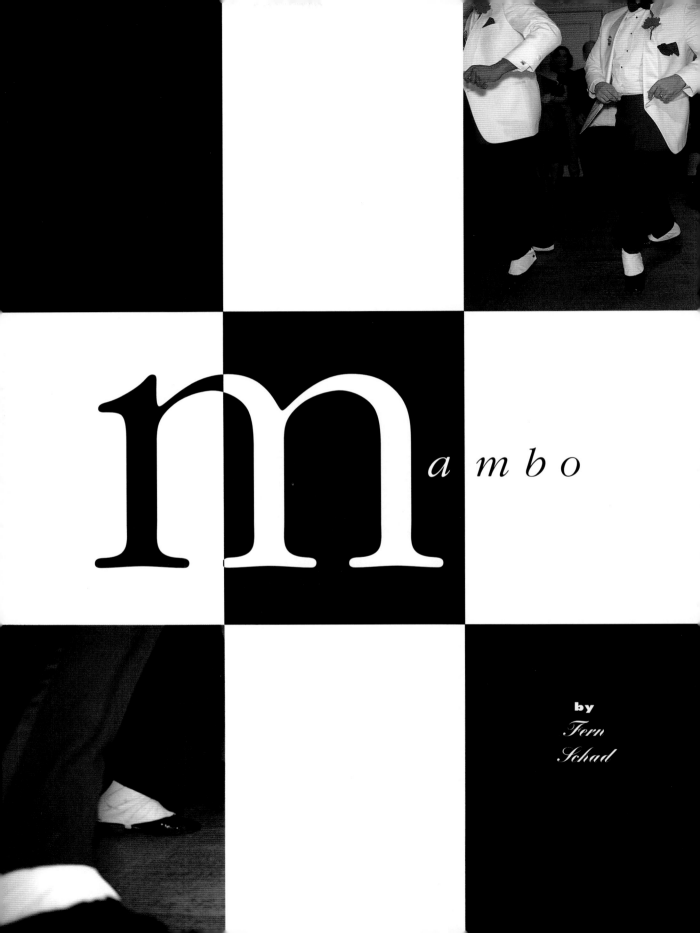

mambo

by

Fern Schad

*M*ambo

Menu

Hors d'Oeuvres
Spiced Crab Cake with Papaya Chutney
Sausage Empanadas
Crudités with Red Pepper Dip

Soup
Sweet Plantain Soup

Entrée
Arroz con Pollo*
Black Beans with Tomato and Onions*
Hearts of Palm Salad
Tomato Pimiento Bread

Dessert
Rum Mousse
Almond Cookies

Mojito Criollo
Cuba Libré
Alsace Gewürtztraminer
Kahlúa con Crema

Chef: Vania Enquist

Hosts:

Deborah and

Peter Krulewitch,

Gillian Jolis,

Andrew Goldstein

*An asterisk denotes that the recipe for the dish is included.

Outside on the street, wintry New York. Inside the front door, the sights and sounds and scents of old Havana. Mojitos (rum, lemon juice, and sugar) to induce the right mood, with crab cakes with papaya chutney, crudités with red pepper mayonnaise, and chorizo empanadas to whet the appetite. Palm fronds, photographs and postcards of old Havana, together with Cuban artifacts, enhanced the atmosphere.

Dinner, on tables laden with fruit arrangements, consisted of plantain soup with plantain crisps, *arroz con pollo,* and black beans garnished with red tomatoes, followed by hearts of palm salad with tomato and cheese bread. The dessert was rum mousse and almond cookies.

After dinner, the mambo! First, an exhibition by the pros. Who would have guessed that hips, legs, and feet could move so fast and so sensuously, accompanied by flashing smiles and without any appearance of effort? After the exhibition, the lessons. Inwardly we groaned as we realized that we guests (rank amateurs) could never measure up. We counted steps as instructed, then swung into action with our hips. Trying to control, let alone coordinate, hips and feet simultaneously was a hard task but we had fun trying. Some of us could even crack a smile without overloading our brains. Those of us who attend aerobics were in better shape than the more sedentary. We put our best foot forward and had a good time, but it's hard to turn proper New Yorkers into even a semblance of subtly swaying Cubans.

We departed the party happy, sore of foot and hip, carrying a bag printed with tropical leaves containing a copy of *The Mambo Kings Play Songs of Love* and a map of Cuba to help us find our way when we go to show off our newfound skills in the land of the mambo's birth.

Party photographs by Mark Jenkinson; still life photograph by Alex McLean

The table decorations, fantasies of fruits and flowers, evoke a Havana that never was (following pages).

Mambo

Arroz con Pollo (Chicken and Rice)

✳

4 boneless chicken breasts, cut in quarters
4 garlic cloves, minced
2 large onions, diced
¼ teaspoon cayenne pepper
1 bay leaf
½ teaspoon paprika
3 tablespoons olive oil
¼ teaspoon saffron
2 cups white rice
4 cups chicken broth
Salt to taste
2 cups white wine
2 cups peeled, seeded, and diced plum tomatoes
1 green bell pepper, seeded and diced
1 10-ounce package frozen peas
1 red bell pepper, seeded and cut in strips
Chopped parsley

1. Marinate the chicken breasts with the garlic, half the diced onion, cayenne pepper, bay leaf, and paprika for at least 4 hours, or overnight if possible.

2. In a large saucepan, heat 1 tablespoon oil over medium heat. Add the saffron. Sauté about a minute, then add the rice and sauté until all the rice is separated. Add the chicken broth, lower the heat, and let it simmer until all the broth is gone. The rice should be cooked by then; if not, add about ½ cup hot water and let it cook off. Salt to taste.

3. In a large saucepan over medium heat, sauté the chicken breasts (2 or 3 at a time) for about 5 minutes on each side, or until they are light brown. Set aside in the same saucepan. Sauté the remaining diced onions for 5 minutes, or until translucent. Then return the chicken breasts to the pan, add the white wine, chopped tomatoes, and green pepper, and let it cook for 10 to 15 minutes. Add the frozen peas and cook for an additional 5 minutes.

4. Place the chicken breasts on top of a bed of rice in a large serving bowl. Garnish with the strips of red pepper and the chopped parsley.

Serves 6 to 8

Black Beans with Tomato and Onions

✻

1 pound dried black beans
2 large onions, diced
1 pound plum tomatoes, peeled, seeded, and
 diced
1 tablespoon olive oil
3 garlic cloves, crushed
Salt and pepper to taste

1. Place the beans in hot water to cover and let them soak at room temperature for 4 to 6 hours.

2. Drain the beans in a strainer and rinse in cold water. Place them in a large pot with enough cold water to cover. At high temperature bring to a boil, add a quarter of the diced onions, lower the heat to medium, and let cook for 1 hour, or until the beans are tender. Add more water if necessary.

3. While the beans are cooking, place the tomatoes in a large bowl and cover with boiling water. Let sit for 4 to 5 minutes, drain, peel, dice, and set aside

4. In a large saucepan, heat the olive oil. Add the garlic and a quarter of the onions. Sauté for 4 to 5 minutes, or until the onions are translucent. Add the beans and salt and pepper to taste. Lower the flame and let it cook for 15 to 20 minutes.

Oscar Hijuelos, author
of Mambo Kings Play Songs of Love, *was a special guest (top), as were the dazzlingly dressed mambo music makers (above and opposite).*

5. Place the beans in a serving bowl, and garnish with the diced tomatoes and the remaining diced onions.

Serves 6 to 8

Mambo

feasting

in

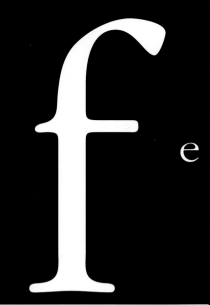

babylon

by

Dorothy
Cullman

Feasting in Babylon

Menu

Appetizer
Pigeon Pie with Pistachios

Entrée
Couscous with Lamb and Chicken*
Mixed Green Salad
with Croutons and Chèvre

Dessert
Mélange of Exotic Fruit
Lemon Sorbet in Lemon Shell
"Lion" Cookies
Moroccan Mint Tea

Assorted Wines

Chef: Glorious Food

*An asterisk denotes that the recipe for the dish is included.

Hosts:

Mr. and Mrs.

Lewis

Cullman

One day in July after I had agreed to give a party for Tables of Content, I was reading about Mesopotamia and Babylon, and I decided it was a good theme for a party—Feasting in Babylon. I called my friend Sidney Babcock, curator of Mr. and Mrs. Jonathan Rosen's fabulous collection of early Middle Eastern cylinders and stamp seals. I asked about ancient recipes, and he said he had a few.

But I also heard mixed reviews from a nearby university that had attempted to use ancient recipes for a party. They were so mixed that I called Glorious Food instead to find out what they had done on Middle East cuisine. Not only had they put on many Arabian nights (semi-compromised for today's taste), but they could also supply musicians and high-style dancing girls. We decided on a first course of pigeon pie; a second course of couscous with lamb, chicken, and veggies; a goat cheese salad; and a dessert of fruit sorbet with Library Lion cookies. (I did not ask how they made sorbets in the Middle East in those far-off days.)

My heart at rest, I moved on to the decor. A talented young woman, Melanie Danza of Pound Ridge, N.Y., had painted some furniture for me. Sidney Babcock gave us some color photographs of museum restorations. Melanie took some seals and Sidney's designs of lions and had them cast into large napkin rings. Unfortunately, she left the painting of them until the last minute, so there were lots of blue hands and blue napkins, but nobody seemed to mind. She abstracted the color designs into two wonderful tablecloths of heavy linen. They were a smash hit on the tables, along with the untouchable napkin rings.

On the night of the dinner, Sidney arrived with a pocketful of seals dating from 3000 to 1000 B.C. He rolled out pieces of soft clay with a rolling pin, used the seals to make an impression, then baked them in a toaster and gave them to our guests. In early days, Sidney explained, these seals were "a form of personal identity, an amulet, a credit card, and a passport, all rolled into one."

After dinner two girls performed dances of the Middle East—only semibelly. They had studied Eastern dance and were knowledgeable as well as beautiful.

My husband and I have a number of antiquities around our apartment, so they added an extra touch of the past to the evening's atmosphere. One guest asked me if these would all have to go back the next day, but I assured him that they were really ours.

Party photographs by Jeanne Trudeau; still life photograph by William Waldron

Couscous with Lamb and Chicken

✳

1 cup dried chick-peas or 1 (20-ounce) can
  cooked chick-peas
4 cups couscous (1½ pounds)
2 pounds lamb shoulder, boned and trimmed
  of fat, cut in 1½-inch pieces
1 whole chicken, cut into 10 pieces
¾ cup sweet butter (1½ sticks), plus butter for
  tossing
2 tablespoons salt
1 tablespoon freshly ground black pepper
Pinch of pulverized saffron
½ teaspoon ground turmeric
2 medium yellow onions, quartered
2 cinnamon sticks (optional)
1 small bundle herbs (green coriander and
  parsley sprigs tied together)
4 or 5 red, ripe tomatoes, peeled, seeded, and
  quartered
1 pound carrots
1 pound turnips
1 pound zucchini
½ pound pumpkin
Flour, for dusting
Handful of black raisins

1. Soak the dried chick-peas overnight.

2. The next day, drain the chick-peas, cover with fresh cold water, and cook, covered, for 1 hour. Drain, then cool and remove the skins by submerging the chick-peas in a bowl of cold water and gently rubbing them between the fingers. The skins will rise to the surface of the water. Discard them and set aside the peeled

chick-peas. (If you are using canned chick-peas, peel them and set them aside.)

3. To prepare the couscous, wash it in a large shallow pan by pouring 12 cups of water over the grain. Stir quickly using your hand, and then drain off excess water through a sieve. Return the couscous grains to the pan, smooth them out, and leave to swell for between 10 and 20 minutes. After roughly 10 minutes, begin, with cupped wet hands, to work the grains by lifting up handfuls of grain, rubbing them gently and letting them fall back into the pan. This process should break up any lumps that may have formed.

4. To prepare the broth, place the meat and chicken in the bottom of a couscousiere with half the butter, the salt, pepper, saffron, turmeric, onions, cinnamon sticks, herbs, and tomatoes. Cover and cook gently over low heat for 10 minutes, giving the pan a swirl from time to time. Then add 3 to 4 quarts of water and the drained chick-peas (if using canned chick-peas, do not add until 30 minutes before serving) and bring to a boil. Simmer 1 hour, covered.

5. Meanwhile, prepare the vegetables: Scrape the carrots and turnips and cut them into 1-inch lengths. Cut the zucchini into quarters. Peel and cut up the pumpkin.

6. Dampen a strip of cheesecloth, dust it with flour, and twist into a strip the length of the circumference of the rim of the bottom part of the couscousiere. Use this to seal the perforated top or colander on top of the pot. Check all sides for effective

sealing: The perforated top should not touch the broth below. Slowly dribble one quarter of the swollen couscous grains into the steamer, allowing them to form a soft mound. Steam 5 minutes and gently add the remaining couscous. When all the grains are in the steamer, lower heat to moderate and steam 20 minutes. Do not cover the couscous while it steams.

7. Remove the top part of the couscousiere (or the colander). Dump the couscous into a large shallow pan and spread out with a wooden spoon. Sprinkle ½ to 1 cup cold water and 1 teaspoon salt over the grains. Separate and break up lumps by lifting and stirring the grains gently. Oil your hands lightly and rework the grains—this helps to keep each grain separate. Smooth the couscous out and allow it to dry for at least 10 minutes. If the couscous feels too dry, then add another cup of water by handful sprinkles, and rake the couscous well before each addition. If you are preparing the couscous in advance, let it dry and cover it with a damp cloth. It can wait hours.

8. Add the carrots and turnips to the lamb broth. Continue cooking 30 minutes more. (The broth has now cooked 2 hours, so add more water if necessary.) To this point the dish can be prepared in advance.

9. Thirty minutes before serving time, cook the pumpkin, in a separate pan, in lamb-flavored water until tender. Add the zucchini and raisins (and canned chickpeas if using them) to the lamb broth. Bring to a boil, reseal the two containers with cheesecloth, and steam the couscous in the top part of the couscousiere for another 20 minutes. Dot the couscous with the remaining butter during the last 5 minutes.

10. Dump the couscous onto a serving dish and toss with additional butter. Use a fork to smooth out any lumps. Spread out and form a large well in the center. With a perforated spoon transfer the meat and vegetables into the well. Add the drained pumpkin. Taste the broth for seasoning and adjust, then strain. Moisten the grain with the strained broth. Serve with Red Pepper Sauce (see below).

Red Pepper Sauce

✳

1 cup lamb broth from the couscous pot
1 teaspoon Harissa sauce (see Note)
1 tablespoon lemon juice
1 to 2 tablespoons olive oil
Pinches of cumin, to taste
Sprinkling of chopped parsley and coriander

Combine all the ingredients in a small saucepan over high heat. Beat well and pour into a small serving bowl.

Note: You can buy tinned Harissa paste from Tunisia at a Middle Eastern grocery or at a gourmet store.

These recipes are adapted from "Couscous and Other Good Food from Morocco" by Paula Wolfert.

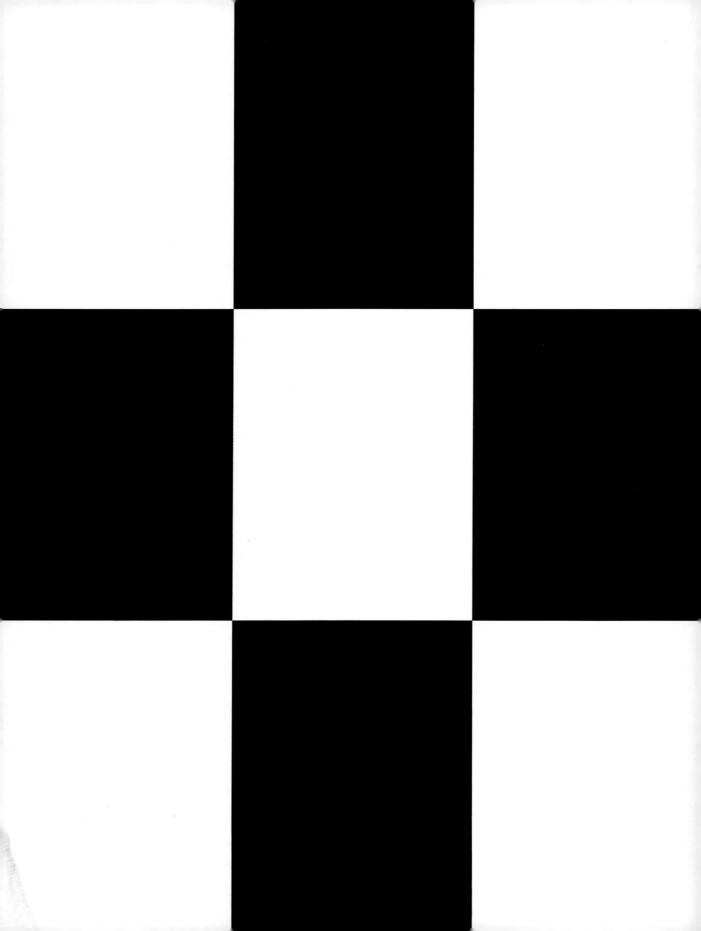

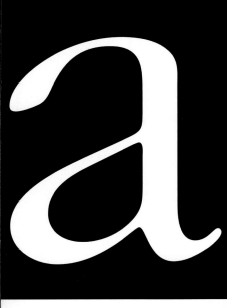

a

masterful

m

eal

by
Kelso Sutton

A Masterful Meal

Menu

Hors d'Oeuvres
Assorted Crudités with Herb Dip
Fresh Oysters
Cheddar Pastry Twists

Appetizer
Sautéed Scallops of Fresh Duck Foie Gras
with Hearts of Curly Endive
and Cracklings

Entrée
Braised Saddle of Veal*
Braised Spinach*
Mushroom Duxelles*
Rice Soubise*

Dessert

Caramelized Pear Tartlets*

Pol Roger Reserve, 1979

Kimich Riesling, 1989

Faiveley Chambertin, 1985

Graham's Port, 1970

Chef: Robert Chambers

Hosts:

Carole and

Frank

Lalli

*An asterisk denotes that the recipe for the dish is included.

*Master chef Julia Child oversees the preparation
of her recipes, enough to cause trepidation in any kitchen staff.
At top right she chats with dinner guest TV critic Joel Siegel. Wine
authority Robert Parker samples one of his selections with Joanna
and Dan Rose. Parker and Child give brief but mouth-watering
talks on their respective subjects. Hosts Carole and Frank Lalli
(bottom right) mingle with their well-fed guests.*

A Masterful Meal

We rode up in the elevator with Barbara Shimkin, who lives above our hosts, Frank and Carole Lalli. She told us her refrigerator was loaded with wonderful bottles of wine for our party. As someone with more than a passing interest in wine, I found this encouraging.

In the Lalli apartment, a quick check of the kitchen revealed three very efficient waiters and four chefs in a blur of activity, shucking oysters and carving saddles of veal. Julia Child began the formal briefing by describing the meal in its entirety as a lovely classic French approach. The menu was definitely a throwback to earlier days— very rich, without the slightest gesture or apology to the light cooking camp.

The sautéed scallops of fresh duck foie gras were very special, rich but not too heavy. The Kimich Forster Ungeheuer Riesling Auslese 1989 that accompanied the foie gras was the high point of the dinner for me. Wine authority Robert Parker explained that the classic wine selection for foie gras is a Sauterne, but he thinks Sauternes have a tendency to be so sweet that they overwhelm the foie gras. For me, the semisweet Kimich was right on. I have been developing a taste for sweet German and Italian wines, and this was a welcome addition to the list.

The braised saddle of veal and accompaniments were everything that one could expect. Parker said he chose the '85 Burgundy "because it was more evolved than the usual '85, so it matched well with the veal, which is always a challenge for me."

Parker talked at some length about Burgundy wines. He pointed out that three-quarters of the top ten wines are Burgundies. The issue of judging how close a Burgundy is to maturity is a minefield. Secondary tastes evolve. If one sees amber and orange at the edge of the wine, it is getting there. But he added that getting there could take a long time. After twelve to thirteen years Burgundy takes on a fruity character; you see new oak; you see new red. He looks for great odors in the wine, like that of Peking duck.

On decanting, Parker said that young wine, under ten to fifteen years, will lose its freshness if decanted too early. He clearly opts on the side of not decanting too early, and I took this to mean something under thirty to sixty minutes.

At this point the port was served. Julia Child raised her concern about a neo-prohibitionist trend, but Parker said he thought the movement had peaked. I had never heard of this movement, but I knew I had peaked and so wended my way home.

Photographs by Sally Phipps

Braised Saddle of Veal (Selle de Veau Braisée à l'Ancienne)

✳

Saddle of veal is tailor-made for a large VIP dinner party since it will serve sixteen to eighteen people luxuriously, and it is relatively easy to cook and carve. The saddle is the double loin—the whole of the small of the back; it contains the backbone with two loin strips on top, and the two tenderloins underneath. It is one of the most expensive cuts of meat around, and you will have to order it from a specialty market since it is far from an everyday morsel. Speaking of luxury prices, however, think how much it would cost to take those sixteen VIP guests to a restaurant, even a relatively modest one at that!

1 15-pound trimmed bone-in saddle of veal, minus kidneys
3 to 4 tablespoons soft unsalted butter
Seasonings: salt, pepper, thyme
10 to 12 strips fresh pork fatback, about 8 by 1½ inches and ⅛ inch thick (or thick-sliced bacon simmered 10 minutes in 2 quarts water, rinsed in cold water, drained, and dried)
Fresh cooking oil for browning the meat
1 cup each roughly chopped carrots and onions, sautéed in 1 tablespoon oil until tender and lightly browned
1 cup dry Madeira or Port
1 cup veal or chicken stock

Sauce
2 tablespoons cornstarch blended with 2 tablespoons Port or Madeira

Special Equipment Suggested
White cotton string
Heavy-bottomed covered roaster (or deep roasting pan and a cover of some sort, such as a pastry sheet and weight)
Instant meat thermometer

1. Dry the saddle with paper towels, and rub all over with the soft butter.

2. Turn it over and season the tenderloins (which run underneath the length of the backbone on each side), dusting them lightly with salt, pepper, and thyme.

3. Cover the tenderloin with strips of pork fat, and fold the flank ends over them.

4. Tie the saddle around the circumference at 2-inch intervals, to keep flanks and pork strips in place.

5. Brown the meat—15 to 20 minutes—by either filming the roaster with cooking oil and browning the meat on top of the stove, or browning it in a roasting pan under the broiler, turning and basting it with oil.

6. Drain out the browning fat. The dish may be completed in advance to this point.

7. Preheat the oven to 375°F.

(continued on next page)

8. Arrange the saddle top-side up in the roaster, and crisscross the remaining strips of pork fat over it. Scrape the browned vegetables around the meat and pour in the wine. Bring to a simmer on top of the stove, cover the roaster, and set in the lower middle level of the oven.

9. In 10 minutes, or when the wine is bubbling in the oven, turn the oven down to 325°F.

10. Baste the meat occasionally with the juices accumulated in the pan. The veal should cook for about 1¾ to 2 hours and is done when a meat thermometer reads 155°F. to 160°F.—it should be slightly pink when carved, and juicy. Remove the meat to a carving board, cover, and let rest 10 to 15 minutes while you prepare the sauce. (Close the oven and keep it at 325°F. to reheat the meat later.)

11. Prepare the sauce: A delicious amount of aromatic liquid will have collected in the roaster. Scraping up any coagulated juices, drain the liquid along with the vegetables into a sieve set over a saucepan; press the juices out of the vegetables. Add the chicken stock and simmer several minutes, skimming the fat off the surface of the liquid. Carefully correct the seasoning. Off heat, blend in the cornstarch mixture; simmer 2 minutes, stirring.

12. To carve, discard the trussing strings and fat strips.

13. To carve the loin strips (top of meat on either side), rapidly cut straight down the length of the backbone on either side. One by one remove the strips by angling your knife outward against the bone, which is shaped like a shelf. Keeping them in order, cut the meat into slanting crosswise medallions ½-inch thick.

14. Turn the saddle over and remove the two tenderloins, slicing them in the same fashion.

15. Set the bone on a hot platter (brace it with the flank pieces); sliding a long knife under the loin strips, slip them back in place on top of the bone. Pile the tenderloin pieces at the two ends of the platter.

16. Cover and reheat briefly in the oven.

17. To serve, spoon a little of the sauce over the meat to glaze it, and pour the rest into a warm bowl—there will be only a spoonful to moisten each serving.

18. Finally, present the platter to the table, so your guests may admire and enjoy this splendid, rarely seen structure.

Braised Spinach

✳

2 to 3 tablespoons softened butter
1 generous cup chopped cooked spinach
⅓ cup beef or chicken bouillon or heavy
　cream
Salt
Freshly ground pepper
Pinch of nutmeg (optional)
1 tablespoon butter (optional)

1. Half an hour or so before you are ready to serve the dish, melt the softened butter in a heavy-bottomed stainless or nonstick frying pan.

2. When bubbling, blend in the spinach and stir over moderately high heat for a minute or so to evaporate the remaining moisture.

3. When the spinach begins to stick to the bottom of the pan, stir in the beef or chicken bouillon.

4. Lower the heat, season lightly with the salt, pepper, and nutmeg, then cover the pan. Simmer slowly for 5 to 7 minutes, stirring frequently to prevent scorching, until the spinach is tender.

5. Just before serving, if you wish, blend in a tablespoon or so more butter.

Serves 4 to 6

Mushroom Duxelles

✳

Duxelles is a concentrate of mushroom flavor, dry and compact—a quick flavoring for sauces and stews, also for stuffings and braises.

4 cups fresh mushrooms or mushroom stems,
　diced
2 tablespoons butter
2 tablespoons minced shallots or scallions
Salt and freshly ground pepper
2 tablespoons Port or Madeira (optional)

1. By handfuls, twist the mushrooms in the corner of a towel to extract their juices.

2. Heat the butter to bubbling, and sauté the mushrooms in hot butter over moderately high heat, stirring and tossing, until the pieces begin to separate from each other, 3 to 4 minutes.

3. Add the shallots or scallions and sauté a moment more; season to taste.

4. Add the wine, if desired, letting it boil down rapidly to nothing.

5. Serve hot as a side dish.

Yields about ½ cup

Rice Soubise
(Braised Rice and Onions)

✳

A savory accompaniment to roasts, this classic French combination is known as *soubise*. The fact that you can do the main cooking in advance makes it particularly useful for a crowd.

4 cups minced onions
4 tablespoons butter
2 cups raw white rice (long-grain or "par-boiled")
4 cups liquid (water only, or water and chicken broth)
½ cup dry white French vermouth or white wine (optional)
¾ to 1 teaspoon salt, or to taste
1 imported bay leaf
Freshly ground pepper
Optional final additions: several tablespoons softened butter and/or sour cream, heavy cream, and grated Parmesan cheese

Special Equipment Suggested
Heavy-bottomed 4-quart saucepan with cover

1. Cook the onions slowly with the butter in the covered saucepan for 10 to 15 minutes, until almost tender but not browned.

2. Uncover the pan and simmer several minutes to evaporate any excess moisture, then fold in the rice and cook for several minutes, stirring, to coat the grains with the butter.

3. Blend in the 4 cups liquid, vermouth or wine, if desired, and the salt and bay leaf.

4. Bring to a simmer. Stir up once, then cover and let cook at a moderate simmer, without stirring again, for 12 to 15 minutes—until the liquid is absorbed and the rice grains are almost tender. Eat a few to test.

5. Cover the pan and set aside; the rice will finish cooking by itself. The dish may be prepared ahead of time to this point. When cool, cover and refrigerate. To reheat, place the rice in its cooking pan in another larger pan of simmering water; fluff the *soubise* gently with a wooden fork as it warms through.

6. To serve, taste carefully and correct seasoning, fluffing in salt and pepper as needed, and the optional butter, sour cream, heavy cream, and/or cheese.

Caramelized Pear Tartlets

※

When you slice pears just the right way, they fan out most attractively when poached in caramel syrup, and make a lovely dessert perched over a dollop of whipped cream and a crisp sugar cookie or buttery puff pastry. The good thing here is that you may prepare the parts well ahead, and perform only a quick assembly job before serving.

2 cups sugar
Big pinch of salt
⅔ cup water
1 cup additional water, more as needed
3 ripe unblemished pears—Boscs have worked
   best for me here

For Serving
6 oval sugar cookies, 1½ by 6 inches, or 2- by
   3½-inch puff pastry rectangles
2 cups lightly sweetened whipped cream

1. To make caramel syrup, blend the sugar, salt, and ⅔ cup water in a heavy 6-cup saucepan and bring to a simmer, swirling the pan until the sugar has completely dissolved and the liquid is perfectly clear.

2. Cover the pan tightly and boil over moderate heat as the syrup thickens and finally begins to darken to a pale walnut color. Remove from heat and let cool several minutes.

3. Then—careful here in case of a boil-over—pour in the additional cup of water, which will at first bubble up as it hardens the caramel; simmer, stirring, to reliquefy the caramel into a syrup. Pour it into a 10-inch frying pan and set over very low heat to keep warm while preparing the pears.

4. Halve, core, and peel the pears. Place each pear half cut-side down and make 5 or 6 lengthwise slices starting ½ inch from the small end, so that the slices will fan out as they cook but stay attached.

5. Place cut-side down in the syrup, which should come at least halfway up; add a little water if needed. Simmer slowly, basting frequently, until the pear slices are tender when pierced with the point of a knife—be sure they are really tender; taste to be sure.

6. Carefully remove them to a nonstick surface. Boil down the syrup until thick enough to coat a spoon lightly, and reserve. (Leftover syrup may be used again, or boiled down with heavy cream to make an excellent caramel sauce.)

7. To serve, place a cookie or the bottom of a puff pastry on each dessert plate (setting the pastry top at the side), spread with a coating of caramel, top with a big spoonful of whipped cream, and drape a pear nicely over each.

a S

ingular

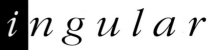

dinner

by
Liz
Smith

A Singular Dinner

Menu

Hors d'Oeuvres
Croutons with Tapenade
Focaccia with Goat Cheese and
Two-Color Tomato

Buffet
Grilled Vegetables Parmigiano

American Cassoulet

Shrimp and Squid Sautéed with Tomato
Brunoise, Capers, Olives,
and Fresh Herbs

Chef Gary Shaw's
Farfalle in Pesto Cream Sauce*

Mesclun with Shallot Vinaigrette

Host:

Robert

Woolley

Dessert
Fresh Pineapple and Blueberries
in Port
Seasonal Fruit Pies

Trefethen Chardonnay, 1990

Nuits-St. Georges, Clos des Corvées, 1987

Chef: Gary Shaw

*An asterisk denotes that the recipe for the dish is included.

robert Woolley is at the heart of the Sotheby's auction experience in this town, and he is a notable "single" about New York, being unabashedly gay, generously philanthropical, and a wonderful "extra man" in the bargain. So it's no wonder that when people were dreaming up different kinds of Tables of Content, Woolley decided it would make for an amusing dinner to help the New York Public Library by mixing a cocktail of various types of "singles" in his own single-man East Side apartment.

Woolley rounded up an assortment of elegant gentlemen plus the recently separated, the long divorced, the widowed, and the "still looking." Everybody dressed up to the nines. There was the dying-to-date-again Kathy Steinberg, vivacious in her new short Scaasi satin dress with a raspberry sherbet bodice and flared short green skirt. There was the perfect pocket Venus, Anne Bass, a catch if there ever was one. Also, along came the great PR maven Eleanor Lambert, who oversees the Best-Dressed List.

I came with the handsome ad man Peter Rogers, whose "What Becomes a Legend Most" mink ads have fallen on difficult times from the animal-rights activists. Noted was the archaeologist Iris Love, who looked Dior-ish and far removed from the shorts and pith helmet of her Turkish dig. Fran Lebowitz was in her de rigueur tuxedo and high-heeled black pumps. I chatted with the British agent Lionel Larner, who can always tell us what Diana Rigg is up to these days. And also in the party were the first Mrs. William Paley, Dorothy Hirshon, the richly bedecked Lyn Revson, the always philanthropic Jan Cowles, and that major domo-turned-cook-book-writer Mark Simpson. Let's not forget the art-minded Peter Bacanovic, the financier Stephen Schwarzman, the decorators Charles Kreusun and Justin Baxter, the Greek beauty Kaliope Karella, and Chanel CEO Michael Rena.

Everybody came on time and gravitated first to Woolley's aviary, which is done up like a tropical jungle with all manner of exotic winged creatures, some flying free. He has quail scurrying on the floor, finches galore, and at least one magnificent blue and gold macaw. A few guests with Alfred Hitchcock hangovers hated this room and rushed right out. The usual ornithological comments were made: "I hate birds . . . I am afraid of birds . . . I love birds . . . What does it cost to keep these?" and "A bird in the house means death!"

The Library had selected for our pièce de résistance the admirable personage of Quentin Crisp, the creator of *The Naked Civil Servant* and a man now writing a column for *The Native*, in which he refers to people as Mr., Miss, Mrs., using only their last names. (This makes for heady and piquant celebrity journalism.) We took turns sitting at Crisp's knee as he presided in a large armchair. We were hoping to discover his "take" on single life. Generally, his attitudes are excellent and upbeat. Evidently,

Tables of Content

Decorated for Christmas, Robert Woolley's apartment is a
visual treat, from tabletop treasures to the ceiling-high tree, and the buffet is laden
with seafood, cassoulet, pasta, and dessert.

A Singular Dinner

everything since his English growing up has been sheer gravy for Crisp. He says, "New Yorkers are so nice and so embracing. They want you to have a good time."

I tried to engage him in a serious discussion about upgrading his standard of living (he resides in a sordid building downtown and lives in appalling penury, as documented in a recent film, *Resident Alien*). Crisp, however, said he did not mind living below the poverty line. "One has to be careful and not run out of money before one runs out of one's life. I have very little money and I have to watch it." I was about to embark on a project to sweeten his mode through contributions when Woolley announced that my time was "up," and I was replaced by Ms. Lebowitz. A discussion about Gloria Swanson began as I departed for the buffet table.

We were offered a lively dinner prepared by an all-American chef named Gary Shaw. He gave us a groaning board cassoulet made up of Southern black-eyed peas instead of the usual French beans, and a pesto pasta.

Throughout the evening, as we shifted from chair to chair and from room to room, a young man played a portable piano. Woolley had bought his services in a previous charity auction. "I thought tonight would be a good time to collect," said Woolley, smiling.

The entertainment came in the form of Christopher Mason with four special songs. First, he sang a paean to the host, "Wild and Woolley." Then he performed a tribute to our guest of honor, "The Quentin Crisp Song." Finally, Mason ended with two bombshell society topicals, as I like to call them, "The Kennedy Trial" and "The Kennedy Torpedo Libido." Instead of his usual birthday posies, this time Mason went to the satiric sardonic edge in his lyrics, proving his wit in hilarious—albeit probably libelous—stanzas ("Teddy is the Senator with lots to teach / Let's spend Easter in Palm Beach").

As I was wending my way home, I decided that I had given the Library my contribution, but the Library had unwittingly given me quite an offbeat and possibly unique evening. Although I didn't meet Mr. Right or even Miss Right at the "singles" dinner, I did decide it is a joy to be single.

Photographs by Terry Gruber

Chef Gary Shaw's
Farfalle in
Pesto Cream Sauce

✳

¾ cup pignoli (pine nuts)
6 tablespoons olive oil
2 medium onions, diced
1 bay leaf
½ pound pancetta (Italian bacon),
   coarsely chopped
1 teaspoon hot red pepper flakes
¼ pound sun-dried tomatoes in oil, julienned
1½ pints heavy cream
1 pound farfalle (bow-tie pasta)
14 ounces pesto
6 tablespoons grated Parmesan cheese

1. Toast the nuts in a dry hot pan by sautéing quickly until brown. Set aside for garnish.

2. Heat the oil in 10-inch pan and sauté the onions with the bay leaf on medium heat until translucent. Add the pancetta and cook briefly until the fat has been rendered. Season with the red pepper flakes, then add the sun-dried tomatoes. Heat through. Discard the bay leaf. Set the mixture aside.

3. In a saucepan bring the heavy cream to a slow simmer and reduce slightly.

4. Meanwhile, cook the pasta in boiling salted water according to the package directions.

5. Five minutes before the desired doneness, skim the skin off the cream and stir in the onion mixture. Heat through until very hot, then add the pesto. (Add the pesto at the last minute to keep the bright green color.)

6. When the pasta is cooked, drain and return to a large pot. Combine the cream sauce with the farfalle. It should be nice and creamy. Stir in the cheese. Garnish with the pine nuts.

Serves 6

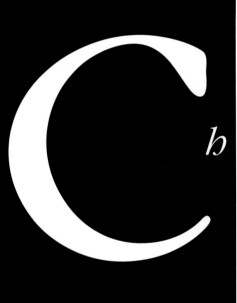

a Chef's story

story

by
Judith Segal

A Chef's Story

Menu

Appetizers
Shoalwater Bay Oysters
Salad of *Frisée* with Walla Walla
Onions and Chanterelles

Entrée
Roast Rack of Lamb
Smothered in Rosemary*
Creamed Hash Brown Potatoes
Timbale of Cabbage

Dessert
Cream Biscuits* with Fresh Berries

Staglin Chardonnay, 1989
El Molino Pinot Noir, 1987
Château Lafaurie-Peyraguey, 1978

Chef: Larry Forgione

Hosts:

Judith Segal, left,

and Barry Michael

Gaines, M.D.,

right

*An asterisk denotes that the recipe for the dish is included.

from start to finish it was a sentimental journey. A group of friends and admirers of the late James Beard agreed that there could be no more fitting memorial to him than a gala dinner in his memory to benefit the Library.

In matters of food, James Beard was a great originator. He was the first to celebrate America's vast and varied natural bounty. He was the original columnist for *Gourmet,* our first magazine to focus on gastronomy, and the first consultant to the famed Four Seasons restaurant and to Sherry-Lehmann Wines. He was a caterer, a cooking teacher, and an author of cookbooks decades before Julia Child became a household name. He was also a man of letters who loved good writing.

My cohost, Barry Michael Gaines, M.D., and I asked Barbara Kafka to be guest of honor. She is one of the leading scholars of the food community, a columnist for both *Vogue* and the *New York Times,* and author of *The Microwave Gourmet.* Even more important, she was Beard's closest friend.

Beard must have had a mischievous streak, because dozens of people will confide that each was his one true friend, and that anyone else who makes that claim is self-deluded. But when asked about Barbara Kafka, all these "best friends" concede that perhaps they were merely Beard's "second-best friend"—after Barbara.

We also asked Chef Larry Forgione to create the dinner. According to Barbara Kafka, Larry was like a son to Beard. Larry's children called Beard "Grandpa." Larry

Forgione is a consultant to leading hotels and restaurants as well as proprietor of the highly respected restaurant An American Place. Beard himself chose the name because it described the philosophy of cooking that he imparted to Larry.

My cohost selected the wines with the help of Michael Aaron, nephew of the founder of Sherry-Lehmann, Beard's early client. I arranged for flowers, linens, candles, and good bread, hired waiters, and made certain there were sufficient and appropriate glasses for the many wines.

We held the dinner at Beard's own home, a Greenwich Village town house that, on his death, was incorporated by his friends as The James Beard Foundation. It has become a living museum for the food industry, with membership open to all.

the night of the dinner, docents led our guests through the thoroughly idiosyncratic building. The entrance leads from Beard's office, which has a window just below ground level, facing Twelfth Street. By one of those mysterious coincidences, Twelfth Street is home to many food writers. Beard was notorious for recognizing his friends' feet as they passed his window. If they went by without stopping to chat, they would hear about their failure from Beard.

The kitchen, predictably, is the center of the house, and it leads to a greenhouse where Beard used to seat guests and students for meals. Then up a flight of stairs to

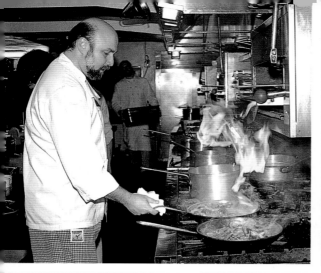

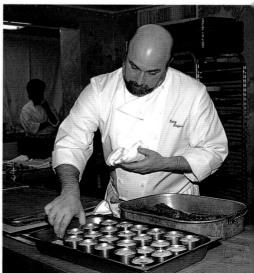

The day of the dinner begins early for Chef Larry Forgione (top left), who starts preparation in the kitchen of his restaurant, An American Place, then loads his car with provisions to be moved to the dinner site. Work begins in earnest in the kitchen of Beard's house— shucking oysters, tossing salad, burying the lamb under sprigs of rosemary, baking Beard's famous biscuits. Plates are carefully arranged before dinner is served in the Beard library. Special guest food writer Barbara Kafka (bottom right) reminisces about her dear old friend.

a glass-enclosed balcony with a shower head and drain, where Beard like to bathe at one with nature—and in front of hundreds of neighbors in adjacent high-rises. Next to the balcony is the salon where Beard hosted scores of entertainments. Barbara Kafka told our guests that Beard had chosen this shade of orange paint because it flatters women.

Larry Forgione's dinner contained all the elements of Beard's thesis of fine cooking: top-quality seasonal and regional ingredients prepared with care, imagination, and simplicity. The wines complemented each dish.

While Larry's food was the clear star of the evening, the champagne was a special highlight. Barry Gaines had secured the last-known six bottles of Champagne Rothschild Cremant 1921, the champagne vintage of the century. As Barbara Kafka advised, the taste and condition of this seventy-year-old wine were irrelevant. She urged us to sample it with historic perspective. While the liquid still bubbled, it was sharp and bitter with a golden-brown color, but we all knew that we were drinking a drop of history.

James Beard would have loved the occasion.

Cooking and party photographs by Mary Hilliard; still life photographs by Jerry Ruotolo

Special thanks: Wines personally selected by Michael Aaron of Sherry-Lehmann Wine Merchants. Smiles from Clayton Triplette. Sparkling water donated by San Pellegrino. Coffee contributed by Switzerland's Café La Semeuse. Music provided by The Jazz Forum All-Stars. Use of The Beard House through the cooperation of The James Beard Foundation, Diane Harris Brown, Director.

Roast Rack of Lamb Smothered in Rosemary (from the New James Beard)

✳

The rack consists of one side of the ribs. In young lamb, or baby lamb, when the ribs have been well trimmed, all excess fat removed, and the fat scraped from the bones (or, in the butcher's term, "frenched"), the rack will consist of six to seven delicate small chops, a perfect piece of meat for two people.

Ask the butcher to cut through the chine bone so that you can carve right through the chops without having to struggle with the bones. If you want to put little paper frills on the rib ends after the rack is cooked, protect the bone ends by twisting pieces of aluminum foil around each one before roasting. A rack of lamb should always be roasted at a high temperature and served rare.

1 rack of lamb, 6 to 7 chops, trimmed of all but about ⅓ inch of fat, with the bones "frenched"
Salt and freshly ground black pepper
1 garlic clove, peeled and crushed
1 teaspoon dried rosemary or thyme, crushed in a mortar

1. Preheat the oven to 450°F. Rub the rack of lamb well with the salt, pepper, garlic, and rosemary or thyme. Twist pieces of aluminum foil around the bone ends.

2. Put the roast, fat side down, on a rack in a roasting pan. Roast for 15 minutes, then turn it over so the bone side is down. Reduce the heat to 400°F. and roast 5 minutes more. Test the meat by pressing it lightly with your fingers, protecting them with paper towels. The meat should feel firmly springy to the touch. If it seems to need more cooking time, return to the oven for a further 5 to 7 minutes. It should take 20 to 27 minutes for rare lamb. The internal temperature, tested with a meat thermometer, should be 125° F to 130° F.

3. Remove the cooked meat to a carving board; substitute paper frills for the foil (if you like to gnaw the little bones, this prevents your fingers from getting greasy). Let it stand 3 minutes, then carve. There are two ways to carve rack of lamb. The more usual is to separate the chops by cutting between the bones and serving 2 or 3 chops to each person, according to appetite. The other way is to carve the meat in long, thin slices parallel to the bone. If you serve the rack that way, serve each person 1 or 2 of the tiny bones to gnaw on.

Serves 2 or 3

Cream Biscuits

(from Beard on Bread *)*

✳

We had a reputation at home for very special biscuits, which were made by our Chinese cook, who was with us for many years. After he left us they became a standard item in our household, and I still make them very often. The secret of their unique quality is this: They use heavy cream instead of butter or shortening.

2 cups all-purpose flour
1 teaspoon salt
1 tablespoon double-acting baking powder

2 teaspoons granulated sugar
¾ to 1 cup heavy cream
Melted butter

Preheat oven to 425°F. Sift the dry ingredients together. Fold in the heavy cream until the soft dough can be easily handled. Turn onto a floured board, knead for about 1 minute, then pat to a thickness of ½ to ¾ inch. Cut in rounds or squares, dip in melted butter, and arrange on a buttered baking sheet. Bake for 15 to 18 minutes and serve hot with fresh berries and whipped cream.

About 12 biscuits

A truly American feast: salad greens with onions from Washington State, roast lamb with potatoes and cabbage timbales, and most indigenous of all, strawberry shortcake with whipped cream, served with James Beard's classic biscuits.

A Chef's Story

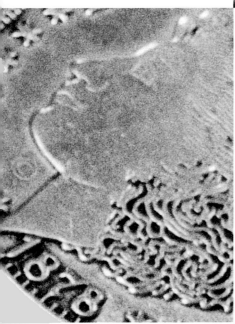

a

magical

e

vening

by

Arlene Fischer

A Magical Evening

Menu

Hors d'Oeuvres
Swedish Caviar on Tiny Potatoes
with Crème Fraîche

Appetizer
Tracy Davis's Mélange of
Wild Mushrooms in Red Wine Sauce*

Entrée
Stuffed Veal Filets with Pignoli and
Watercress Sauce
Wild Rice with Currants and Scallions
Haricot Vert Bundles
Mesclun, Lamb's Lettuce, and Mâche in
Lime Vinaigrette

Dessert
Chocolate Chestnut Bûche de Noël with
Chestnut Truffles

Acacia Chardonnay, 1988

Château Gruaud-Larose, 1978

Tattinger, 1983

Chef: Tracy Davis

*An asterisk denotes that the recipe for the dish is included.

Hosts:

Alan and

Kathy

Greenberg

It was billed as A Magical Evening at Alan and Kathy Greenberg's house. No sooner did guests step into the stunning apartment overlooking Central Park than, indeed, they were whisked into the world of legerdemain. Kathy, looking enchanting in champagne-colored satin pants and jacket, immediately led her visitors to the sumptuous library, where two magicians, Jerry Deutsch and David Roth, presented their beguiling sleights of hand. In the blink of an eye tiny hankies grew into flowing scarves, playing cards mysteriously disappeared and reappeared, a single coin became five quarters, and a Kennedy dollar grew ten times in size. Before the second sip of cocktails everyone was "hooked"—sophisticated, skeptical New Yorkers standing around in tight little circles exclaiming and laughing over the impossible.

It was a smallish gathering, six couples in addition to the Greenbergs, ranging in age from thirtysomething to over seventy. There is always an element of surprise (spell that *r-i-s-k*) when a party is put together by an unseen hand. But everyone mingled happily. When you place a Wall Street leader, an oil company magnate, a couple of real estate tycoons, a major retailer, some well-respected lawyers, and writers in the same room, you'll hardly encounter a wall of silence. The invitation called for festive dress, prompting the women to choose elegant short dresses or dinner suits mostly in black velvet or silk, although there were touches of hot pink

and red as well. The men, of course, wore the uniform of choice—dark business suits and white shirts.

As for host Alan, otherwise known as "Ace," you never know what tricks this amateur magician has up his sleeve—although, as he explains, "Dogs do tricks. I do miracles!" Entertaining right along with the pros, he "disappeared" a guest's diamond and ruby ring, only to have it turn up seconds later in a zippered case he pulled from his pocket. Alas, it didn't increase tenfold in size like the Kennedy dollar.

The magicians continued their conjuring throughout the cocktail hour while waiters served delicious tiny potato canapés filled with crème faîche and caviar. Someone asked Kathy if she found the magic routines old hat. "Oh, no," she said, laughing. "I'm Alan's biggest fan."

around nine o'clock dinner was served in the grand dining room, decorated for the occasion with dangling silvery moons and stars. The meal began with an elegant appetizer of sautéed chanterelles, morels, and other lush mushrooms followed by scrumptious stuffed filets of veal. Between bites and sips of red or white wine, the talk centered on the economy, New York City real estate, Kathy's career as a pro bono lawyer, and, of course, the latest nationally televised rape case. Midway through dinner, guest Robert Fischer offered a toast: "There is indeed magic in the air at this splendid gathering. We thank you for your gracious hospitality."

Following coffee and dessert, everyone settled in the living room for the main event, a dazzling display of magic by world-renowned conjurer Eric DeCamps. The audience was warmed up by two miracles performed by Ace, and then Eric amazed all of us with thimbles, balls, and coins—beautiful sleight of hand. It's safe to say that many in the savvy audience were watching for the slightest slipup that would reveal the reality behind the magic. No luck. The finest magicians, it seems, never let things out of the hat.

But do magicians ever intentionally reveal their secrets? Alan recalls that his mother once said to him, "Before I die could you please tell me how you do at least one trick?" Alan's reply was an enigmatic smile.

Photographs by Tim Clary

Tracy Davis's Mélange of Wild Mushrooms in Red Wine Sauce

✳

8 large porcini mushrooms
½ pound shiitake mushrooms
½ pound oyster mushrooms
½ pound parasol mushrooms
½ pound morel mushrooms
½ pound chanterelle mushrooms or puffball
    mushrooms
3 tablespoons olive oil
1 cup (2 sticks) unsalted butter
4 scallions (green included), minced
2 garlic cloves, minced
½ pound grated Gruyère
½ cup grated Parmesan
½ cup minced Italian parsley
½ cup chopped walnuts
Freshly ground pepper
¾ cup red wine
½ cup good port

1. Preheat oven to 400°F.

2. Clean all mushrooms with a pastry brush or paper towel, and trim off only woody ends of stems.

3. Heat the olive oil and ¼ cup of the butter in a frying pan. Sauté the scallions until well wilted. Add 1 clove of the garlic and sauté 1 minute (don't burn it). Mix in the Gruyère, Parmesan, parsley, and walnuts. Grind fresh pepper over all and set aside off the heat.

Before dinner, hostess Kathy Greenberg, seated, obliges the magicians by playing straight man as her guests try to see through the sleight of hand.

4. Pack the cheese mixture into the porcini mushroom cavities, stems up. Place the mushrooms in a lightly oiled baking dish. Bake for 10 minutes.

5. While the mushrooms bake, sauté the remaining mushrooms with the remaining clove of garlic in ¼ cup of the butter, for 5 minutes to 7 minutes. Add up to 2 tablespoons more butter if necessary. Remove from the heat when the mushrooms begin to wilt.

6. Remove the porcini from the oven and arrange on a platter (or in 8 individual dishes). Arrange the sautéed mushrooms around the porcini.

7. Pour off fat from the sauté pan. Add the wine and reduce to half over high heat. Add the port and reduce again. As the sauté thickens, swirl in with a whisk the softened remaining butter.

8. Any juices that have accumulated around the mushrooms on the platter can be added to the wine sauce for more flavor.

9. Drizzle the hot sauce over the mushrooms and serve.

Serves 8

A Magical Evening

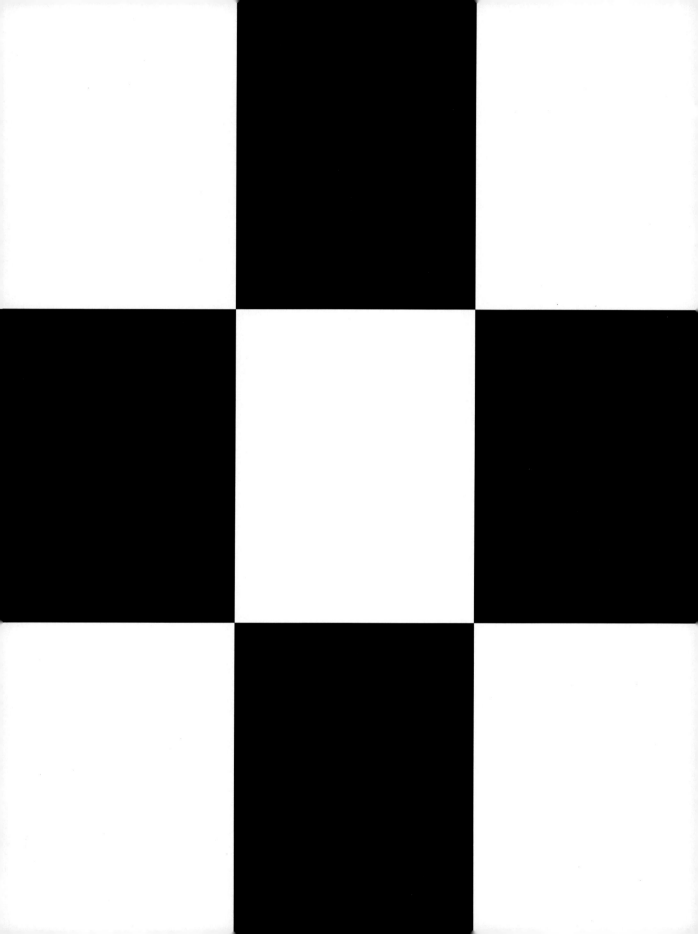

a night of intrigue

by

Tricia Reinus

Night of Intrigue

Menu

Hors d'Oeuvre
Assorted Russian Canapés

Appetizers
Caviar à la Russe
Pepperoni Pizza à la Clancy

Soup
Clear Salmon Soup

Entrée
Beef Stroganov à la Allie Tint*
Salate

Dessert
Cream Puffs with Chocolate Sauce

Perrier Jouët

Chef: Allie Tint

Hostess:

Marchesa Katrin

Theodoli

*An asterisk denotes that the recipe for the dish is included.

the cold crystalline air sparkled around the penthouse windows, reflecting a collage of lights and hubbub far below. The small elegant group chatted while sipping Perrier Jouët champagne and nibbling *zakuski* (Russian canapés). They were surrounded by lush floral arrangements from Maxime's.

The sound of heavy footsteps approaching the door silenced the guests. A man entered the room, his gray hair perfectly in place, an unlighted cigarette between his strong sailor's hands. His tinted glasses reflected the surprise in the guests' faces. He reached into his breast pocket and drew a silver revolver. With a crooked grin, he lifted the glinting weapon to his head and pulled the trigger. Out came a small flame, and he lighted his cigarette. With smoke encircling his head, he said, "Hi, I'm Tom Clancy."

Thus began an evening of intrigue and fun for the dinner hosted by the Marchesa Katrin Theodoli honoring Tom Clancy, best-selling author of *The Hunt for Red October, Patriot Games,* and other spy novels. The Marchesa, CEO of Magnum Marine, a custom builder of super-power yachts, and her ten-year-old son, Giovanni, had long been Clancy fans, as evidenced by the *Hunt for Red October* video games strategically placed throughout the Upper East Side duplex.

Organized by Patrice Tanaka & Company, the evening was dedicated to fantasy, from the table setting to the Russian menu created by Allie Tint's Parties on Fifth. The tone encouraged swapping sea stories and fueling the mutual admiration society between Clancy and Mrs. Theodoli— his books and her boats. Clancy regaled the group with tales from the spy front, admitting that his protagonist Jack Ryan was truly his alter ego.

Dressed in a red crepe dress with a black bow and collar reminiscent of Cossack styles, Mrs. Theodoli rang her guests into the dining room, where they enjoyed a first course of Russian sevruga caviar and, at Clancy's request, pepperoni pizza, his favorite food. The soup course, a clear salmon soup called *Ukha,* was followed by hearty Beef Stroganov à la Allie Tint. Coffee, cognac, and *Moroz Hennoye* (Russian cream puffs glazed with chocolate) set the stage for relaxed conversation. Clancy autographed each guest's complimentary copy of *Sum of All Fears,* as well as other books guests had brought along.

Before the guests left, laden with party bags, young Giovanni Theodoli persuaded Clancy to play a few games of *Hunt for Red October* on the video screen. No one knows who won—that would diminish the intrigue.

Party photographs by Lisa Bogdan; still life photographs by David Fraser

Regal Russian caviar, served at a splendidly set table, was followed by a plebeian
pepperoni pizza, a special request from the guest of honor.

Tables of Content

Special guest thriller writer Tom Clancy poses, appropriately, with pop gun in hand and with his hostess, Katrin Theodoli.

A Night of Intrigue

Beef Stroganov
à la Allie Tint

*

2 pounds filet mignon, cut into thin strips
3 tablespoons unsalted butter
¾ cup finely chopped onion
¾ pounds small fresh white button mushroom
    caps, cleaned and halved
2 ¼ teaspoons all-purpose flour
⅓ cup beef broth
⅓ cup whipping cream
½ cup sour cream
2 teaspoons Düsseldorf or Dijon mustard
1½ tablespoons chopped fresh dill
1½ tablespoons chopped fresh parsley
Salt and freshly ground black pepper to taste

1. Heat a big heavy skillet—we suggest cast iron—over high heat. Add the meat, a few pieces at a time, and quickly sear on all sides, stirring all the time with a wooden spoon, 3 to 4 minutes. If there is an excess amount of liquid, drain and set aside. Remove the meat from the pan and set aside.

2. Melt the butter in a medium-size skillet over medium heat. Add the onions and sauté, stirring frequently until soft, approximately 4 minutes. Raise the heat to medium-high, then add the mushroom caps and sauté, stirring frequently until they are a deep golden brown, 18 to 20 minutes. Turn the heat down to medium-low. Sprinkle in the flour and cook, stirring, for about 1 minute.

3. Stir in the broth, whipping cream, sour cream, mustard, and the meat juices. Simmer over low heat until the sauce thickens, about 5 minutes. Do not boil.

4. Return the meat to the skillet, stir to coat with the sauce, and heat for approximately 1 minute. Stir in the dill, parsley, salt, and pepper, and serve at once.

Serves 6 to 8

Guests were given copies of Tom Clancy's books as favors, and after dinner the guest of honor was kept busy signing them.

a

V*ictorian*

dinner

by
Pamela Scurry

Victorian Dinner

Menu

Appetizer
Smoked Mackerel with Whipped Cream
Horseradish Sauce

Soup
Asparagus Soup

Entrée
Leg of Lamb Served on a Bed of Sage,
Trimmed with Oranges and Grapes
Nutted Rice with Golden
Raisins and Pecans
Italian Medley Eggplant, Tomatoes,
Leeks and Fennel
Endive Salad Served with Pears and
Blue Cheese

Hosts:

Pamela and

Richard

Scurry, Jr.

Dessert
Victorian Flowerpots of Peach Melba
Topped with Meringue and Fresh
White Tulips*

Pinot Grigio
Château de Pressac
Dom Perignon

*An asterisk denotes that the recipe for the dish is included.

the evening was a festive celebration of spring in the middle of winter. In today's world you can serve the freshest asparagus in December. And the freshest of flowers, too—tulips in snowtime.

Before dinner we had champagne in the Victorian greenhouse, where we had placed a white Victorian-style candle in each window. Then downstairs to dinner. Our table had a gold tablecloth with a white antique tablecloth over it. Little crystal Victorian vases were filled with white spring flowers: belled tulips, hyacinths, paperwhites, amaryllis. We used Victorian glasses and antique white napkins with brass floral curtain rings as napkin holders. Place cards with the names written in gold were set in Victorian brass frames. As party favors we gave each guest a brass Victorian frame wrapped in tulled gold lace ribbon.

We have volunteered to host Tables of Content dinners all five years. We always ask the Library to send us guests who have not been to one of our previous dinners. And we tell all our friends to sign up for someone else's dinner. New York is such a fabulous place that we find it more interesting to meet new people whom we might never have encountered in our normal lives. It is one of the special pleasures of Tables of Content.

I wore a white Victorian long dress and my husband, Richard, wore an antique cutaway with striped morning pants. Our young children were also dressed in Victorian style. Our piano player was dressed in—you guessed it!—Victorian attire as he played romantic Victorian love songs.

It was a joyful evening of spring splendor in the winter.

Party photographs by Christopher Little; still life photographs by David Fraser

A Victorian Dinner

*Victorian lace, antique curtain holders used as napkin rings, and place cards
in picture frames make a nostalgic table setting.*

Tables of Content

Victorian Flowerpots
of Peach Melba
Topped with
Meringue and Fresh
White Tulips

✳

10 Small clay flowerpots
Spiced peaches
Raspberry melba sauce
Vanilla ice cream
Meringue (whip together 5 egg whites and
    1¼ cups confectioners' sugar until stiff)
Flowers for garnish

1. First, wash the clay pots in the dishwasher. When they are completely dry, paint them—only on the outside—gold.

2. To make the dessert, fill the bottom of each pot with spiced peaches and then top the peaches with raspberry melba sauce.

3. Add vanilla ice cream, more raspberry sauce, and top the whole thing with meringue.

4. Insert a straw that has been cut in half into the center of each pot. The straw should not show.

5. Bake the pots in a 400° F. oven until the meringue is brown—it should look like soil. This may take only 2 or 3 minutes. If you are making this ahead, put the pots in the freezer now.

6. To serve, either insert a flower into the straw or remove the straw and insert the stem of the fresh flower directly into the hole in the dessert. White tulips, which I used, look particularly pretty and went with my white and gold Victorian theme.

Serves 10

*Cocktails are served in the
Scrurrys' extravagant rooftop
bathroom cum greenhouse (above
right). Dinner progresses to a more
predictable dining room (center)
and is capped by a meringue
dessert, concocted and served by the
hostess herself (bottom right).*

a

night

in

V

ienna

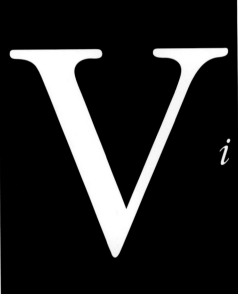

by
Louise Grunwald

𝒜 Night in Vienna

Menu

Appetizer
Smoked Seafood Terrine with
Horseradish Sauce and
Celery Rémoulade

Entrée
Wiener Schnitzel*
Home-Fried Potatoes
Cucumber and Red Onion Salad

Dessert
Apricot *Palatschinken**
Assorted Viennese Cookies

Gruner Veltliner
Schilcher
Blaufrankischer Burgunder

Chef: David Holtquist

Hosts:

Louise and Henry

Grunwald

*An asterisk denotes that the recipe for the dish is included.

there was no *schlag,* but almost every thing else was Viennese: Wiener schnitzel, fiddlers, *palatschinken* (a Central European version of crepes suzette and simply luscious), lots and lots of conversation, and even a few Viennese. Frederic Morton was our star. His marvelous book *A Nervous Splendor* was so enticing that it prompted my first trip to Vienna. I never imagined then that a long time later I would live in that former Imperial capital for two years. Nor did I suspect that I would give a dinner billed as A Night in Vienna and actually be able to pronounce what I was eating and even know a little history of that once powerful city and its enigmatic, contradictory people.

The six hundred—plus years of the Austro-Hungarian empire produced a multitribed population: Hungarians, Bohemians, Poles, Italians. Our evening was a mixed bag as well: a Hungarian, a German, a Swiss-Viennese, an Australian terrier, and of course an American or two. There was even a no-show—a journalist who was trapped in the security net of Salman Rushdie's sudden appearance at Columbia University.

The food was authentic Viennese but produced by an excellent American chef. The wine gushed: a Gruner Veltliner, which is dry, fresh, and comes from the lovely Wachau valley along the Danube near Vienna; a Schilcher from Carinthia, which is a harmless-looking pink but packs a real wallop; and a Blaufrankischer Burgunder,

a rich red from Burgenland, near the Hungarian border.

But the icing of the evening was Fred Morton, who like my husband was born in Vienna and fled in 1938. He reminisced that when he was fifteen years old, on his childhood street, he heard people singing a haunting Viennese song. The words were by Alfred Grunwald, my father-in-law, who wrote many other popular songs still heard on records and in cafés and cabarets all over Central Europe. Fifteen years later in New York, when Morton was awarded a Columbia University graduate fellowship, his parents rewarded him with a gift subscription to *Time* magazine, where my husband, Henry, was a young writer. From then on, Morton said, he regularly encountered the cultural product of the house of Grunwald.

The Viennese talent for making connections, for bringing disparate people together, was further illustrated when Morton read from his latest book, *Thunder at Twilight,* an account of the two years before the outbreak of World War I. The first chapter describes five weirdly assorted men who happen to be in the city during carnival 1913.

There was a slightly foppish Russian émigré who edited a radical paper called *Pravda* and played chess in the Café Central: Leon Trotsky. There was a Georgian revolutionary in peasant boots named Dzhugashvili who would soon attack Trotsky in print under a pseudonym he had just adopted: Stalin. Next, a lusty Croatian auto worker with an eye for the girls called Josip Broz, later known as Tito. Next, Dr. Sigmund Freud, who spent *his* carnival finishing an essay, *Totem and Taboo.*

And finally, a grim loser living in a municipally supported Home for Men who was a failure as a painter but kept on painting when he was not ranting against Jews, Freemasons, and Slavs, or watching *Siegfried* at the opera. His name was Adolf Hitler.

Fred Morton read expressively, and our group visualized these men who would dominate so much of the twentieth century, brought together by chance in the city of odd mixtures and strange encounters.

After Morton stopped reading, we talked long into the night. The coffee was Viennese, but the brandy was French.

Photographs by Bill Helms

Before dinner, guests mingle in the Grunwald living room (top right), including Dr. Timothy Healy, seated, president of The New York Public Library, talking with his hostess. At dinner (bottom right), host Henry Grunwald, former Ambassador to Austria, and for this occasion wearing a traditional Austrian jacket, keeps the wine and the conversation flowing.

Wiener Schnitzel
(Breaded Veal Cutlets)

✳

1 cup flour seasoned with 1 teaspoon salt
   and ½ teaspoon white pepper
2 eggs plus ¼ cup water whisked together
2 cups plain bread crumbs
8 veal cutlets, ⅜ inch thick, pounded flat
4 tablespoons butter
4 tablespoons vegetable oil
2 lemons: 1 cut into slices; 1 cut into
   wedges

1. In three separate shallow bowls, set up your breading station with the flour, egg and water mixture, and bread crumbs.

2. Starting with one piece of veal at a time, dredge with flour, shaking off any excess. Pass through the egg mixture, allowing any excess to drip off. Finally, coat with the bread crumbs, patting firmly.

3. Preheat a sauté pan, add 2 tablespoons of the butter and 2 tablespoons of the oil, and allow the mixture to heat over a medium-high flame. Brown the cutlets. Change the butter-oil mixture as necessary when the crumbs become too brown. Set the cutlets aside until all are browned.

4. The cutlets can be kept in a preheated 400°F. oven for 7 to 10 minutes just before serving. Transfer to a serving tray and place the lemon slices alternately between the cutlets. Place the wedges alongside.

Serves 4 to 6

Apricot
Palatschinken
(Apricot-Filled Crepes)

✳

Crepes
1¾ cups flour (or more)
1 cup milk (or more)
2 teaspoons confectioners' sugar
Pinch of salt
3 eggs
Vegetable oil

Filling
1 cup apricot jam
1 to 2 tablespoons dark rum
1 to 2 tablespoons cognac
Confectioners' sugar

1. Whisk together the flour, milk, sugar, and salt until smooth. You may have to add a little more flour or milk depending on the thickness of crepe you prefer. This crepe is crisper than the French.

2. Whisk in the eggs.

3. Heat a 6-inch sauté pan over medium-high heat, add about 2 tablespoons oil, and heat. Add enough batter to coat the bottom of the pan by rolling from side to side. Allow it to brown slightly, turn, and brown the other side.

4. Remove and proceed with the remaining batter. Stack the crepes with wax paper, separating each one. Keep warm on a covered plate.

5. To make the filling, over medium heat melt the jam with the rum and cognac.

6. Spread a generous tablespoon of jam mixture over each crepe and roll up.

7. Serve with confectioners' sugar sprinkled over the top.

Yields 12 crepes to serve 6

A convivial group enjoys fine Austrian food and wine, and after dinner listens to a reading by author Frederic Morton. Louise Grunwald and Harry, her Australian terrier, pay close attention.

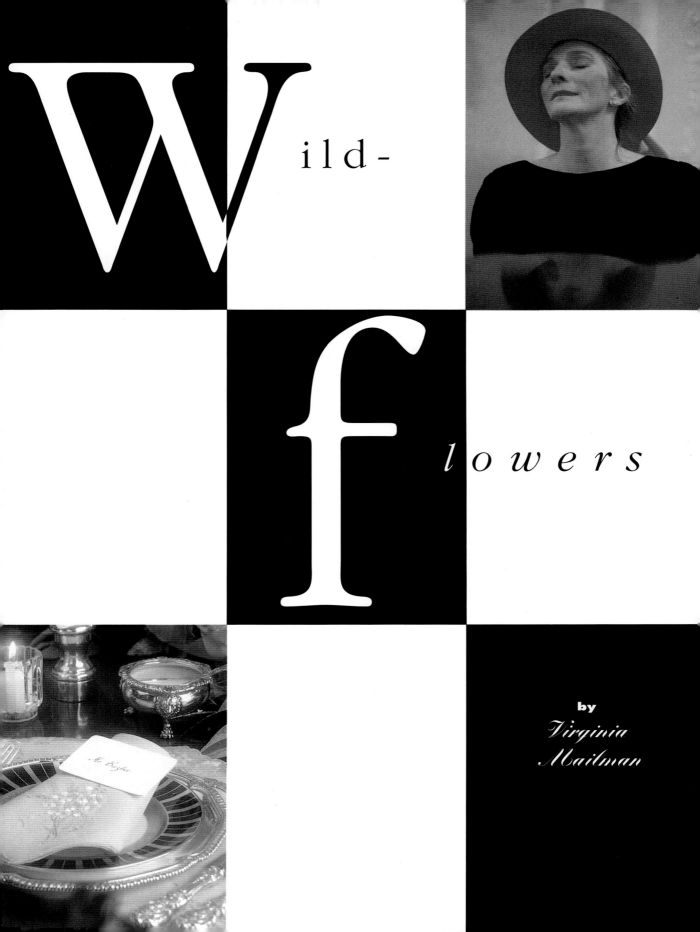

W ild-

f lowers

by
Virginia Mailman

$\mathscr{W}$ildflowers

Menu

Appetizer
Salmon and Sole Watercress Terrine*

Entrée
Roast Loin of Pork Stuffed with Apricots
and Raisins*
Small Roast Potatoes
Glazed Green Vegetables
Carrot Puree in Artichoke Hearts
Endive and Brie Cheese

Dessert
Individual Grand Marnier Soufflés*

Louis Latour Montagny, 1980

Louis Latour Red Burgundy, 1981
Dom Perignon

Chef: Manuela Bogarim

*An asterisk denotes that the recipe for the dish is included.

Hosts:

Virginia and

Norton

Mailman

as a hostess, I love to use flowers, so I called on Kevin Lambert of John Springman, Associates. The dining room table and mantelpiece were covered with more than 300 stems of Hawaiian Blush Dendrobium orchids, ringed with gilded bay leaf roping and gold French ribbon. A three-foot live Stone California pine decorated with gold beads, gold spiral pinecones, and gilded red rose ornaments adorned the console table. In the drawing room, Casablanca lilies and red ilex berries filled a large bowl on the piano. Other arrangements of flowering tulips mixed with pink nerine were scattered around the room.

During cocktails I asked John Buzbee, a guest, if he had ever attended a Tables of Content dinner. He said that two years ago he and his wife had signed up for one, but in the confusion of their return from a European holiday, they thought the dinner was the following evening. They were mortified when the Library called them the next day to ask what had happened. I said, "Funny, but a couple failed to show up here two years ago for exactly the same reason." It indeed turned out that our party was the one the Buzbees had missed.

Edward Pardoe, who sat on my right at dinner, mentioned that he played squash at the Racquet Club. I asked if he knew my son Bruce. He laughed. They had never met before that very morning when they played their first early-morning squash game.

David Rose, the man on my left, is in the computer software business. When I told him I dabbled in writing, he was horrified to discover I had neither fax, nor modem, nor CompuServe. I received all three from him as a thank-you for the evening. In fact, every guest wrote a thank-you note.

After dinner I introduced Judy Collins, singer, composer, author. After coffee in the drawing room, Judy sat at the piano and talked about her background, growing up in Los Angeles and Denver, singing on her father's radio show, her training as a classical pianist who played with the Denver Symphony, and her conversion to folk music. She then played and sang two original ballads, "The Blizzard" and an autobiographical sketch called "My Father." She also sang "Send in the Clowns" and "Both Sides Now," and ended with her traditional rendition of "Amazing Grace." Then she individually autographed copies of the book *Amazing Grace,* for which she wrote the foreword. I thanked her with a clown doll that walked and blew bubbles while playing "Send in the Clowns." I thought it was a splendid evening. Everyone was relaxed and friendly. While all the guests were strangers to one another in the beginning, several wound up exchanging telephone numbers.

Party photographs by Henry Goskinsky; still life photographs by Steve Cohen

The elegant Mailman dining room is awash in Dendrobium orchids and aglow with candlelight from Georgian gilt candelabra. Guest of honor Judy Collins (above center, in hat) is an attraction both at dinner and afterward, when she performs some of her most famous songs. Norton and Virginia Mailman take a moment together before the guests arrive.

Salmon and Sole Watercress Terrine

✳

Salmon Mousse

½ pound salmon fillet
¼ pound sea scallops
1 tablespoon tomato paste
½ teaspoon salt
¼ teaspoon pepper
Pinch of nutmeg
2 cups heavy cream

Sole and Watercress

4 cups watercress leaves, rinsed
½ pound sole fillet
½ pound sea scallops
½ tablespoon salt
Pinch of nutmeg
Pepper to taste
2 cups heavy cream

1. To make the Salmon Mousse, in a food processor puree the salmon and scallops, tomato paste, salt, pepper, and nutmeg until smooth. Add the cream and blend. Transfer to a bowl and refrigerate.

2. To prepare the Sole and Watercress, in a food processor puree the watercress; add the sole, scallops, salt, nutmeg, and pepper; puree. Add the cream and chill.

3. In a well-buttered terrine, spread the Salmon Mousse and Sole and Watercress in layers. Cover with wax paper. Put in a baking pan, add water to the pan, and bake in a 350°F. oven for 45 minutes.

4. Unmold, slice, and serve at room temperature.

Serves 14

Roast Loin of Pork Stuffed with Apricots and Raisins

✳

Stuffing

½ cup bread crumbs
½ cup raisins
2 tablespoons chopped dried apricots
½ cup orange juice
1 egg, lightly beaten
½ teaspoon dried thyme
Dash of cinnamon

3 pounds boneless pork loin

Apricot Sauce

1 cup apricot jam
½ cup water
½ cup sweet butter
½ teaspoon cinnamon
¼ teaspoon ground cloves

1. Mix the stuffing ingredients together and stuff the meat.

2. To make the Apricot Sauce, combine the apricot jam and water and boil until well combined. Add the butter bit by bit with the cinnamon and ground cloves. Whisk until the butter melts, then place in a blender and process until smooth.

Host and Hostess thank Judy Collins for her performance and present her with a cuddly clown doll that plays Judy's famous "Send in the Clowns."

3. Cook the meat on a rack in a 325°F. oven for 2 hours while brushing frequently with Apricot Sauce. Cook for another 30 minutes at 350°F.

Serves 14

Individual
Grand Marnier Soufflés

✳

⅓ cup butter
½ cup all-purpose flour
2 cups milk
4 egg yolks
½ cup Grand Marnier
5 egg whites
¼ cup sugar

1. Preheat the oven to 350°F.

2. Melt the butter over low heat, stir in the flour, and blend well.

3. Add the milk and cook the mixture until thick. Remove from heat.

4. Stir in the egg yolks one at a time, and then add the Grand Marnier.

5. In a separate bowl, beat the egg whites until whipped, and add the sugar. Fold gently into the egg yolk mixture.

6. Fill individual soufflé dishes with the mixture and bake for 25 minutes. Serve immediately.

Makes 14 soufflés

Café gundel

Café

gundel

of Budapest

by
Vera Blinken

Café Gundel of Budapest

Menu

Soup
Palóc Soup à la Gundel Served with
Lagos Pita

Appetizer
Crab Pörkölt *en Cassolette* as
in County Zala

Entrée
Mignons of Venison, Bikavér Sauce
Chestnut Puree
Wild Mushroom Croquettes
Cranberry-Filled Pears

Dessert
Apricot Brandy Sherbet Accompanied
by Apricot Brandy
Pancakes à la Gundel*

Duna Chardonnay, 1988
Egri Bikavér, 1984

Chef: Valeria Matuszka

*An asterisk denotes that the recipe for the dish is included.

Hosts:

Vera and

Donald

Blinken

the theme of the dinner given by myself and my husband Donald, a Library trustee, was to re-create a traditional feast from Budapest's landmark restaurant, Café Gundel.

I was born in Budapest, so the New York-Budapest connection was the result of my friendships with New Yorkers closely identified with Hungarian activities. The current revival of interest in Hungarian customs, cuisine, and culture made our theme an appropriate tribute to the Library's growing Eastern European Research Collection.

In 1991, Ronald Lauder, former ambassador to Austria, and George Lang of the Café des Artistes acquired the old Café Gundel. From its opening in 1894, Gundel's was the center of Budapest's cultural, political, and social life. Unfortunately, during the last forty-five years, the restaurant fell on hard times. But it has now been totally refurbished and it reopened in June 1992. The dinner at our apartment was an opportunity to preview Gundel's famous cuisine. It was the first time that authentic Gundel specialties were served in a private home.

George Lang invited his compatriot Paul Kovi, co-owner of the Four Seasons, to help plan the evening. He also found the right chef for the occasion: Valeria Matuszka was for several years the assistant to Kalman Kalla, the former executive chef of the Hungarian Embassy in Washington and the new executive chef at Café Gundel.

Now the feast! The first course was Palóc Soup à la Gundel, invented by Janos Gundel when he was challenged to improve on the traditional beef-vegetable soup. He created a new Hungarian classic, changing the traditional larding of beef to mutton and adding fresh green beans and sour cream. Presented on our Herend china, it looked as inviting as it tasted. The second course, Crab Pörkölt in pot-shaped *cassolettes,* provided the one crisis of the dinner. I had expected a delivery of fresh crabmeat but received instead several hundred tiny and very much alive crabs! Momentary panic gave way to resolution, and by dinnertime the crabmeat had taken its preordained place in the *cassolettes.*

Mignons of venison marinated for two weeks in Bikavér wine, accompanied by chestnut puree and cranberry-filled pears, was the main dish—served, of course, with Egri Bikavér (the renowned Bull's Blood). This was followed by apricot brandy sherbet and crepes Gundel, a jealously guarded Gundel specialty.

But the food and drinks were, as at all Tables of Content dinners, an accompaniment to guest-raconteurs. After an opening toast from Library Chairman Marshall Rose, George Lang entertained us with a history of Gundel's, along with comments on Hungarian cuisine. Matthew Nimentz described how, as counselor to Secretary of State Cyrus Vance in the late 70s, he had personally carried the crown of St. Stephen's, Hungary's national symbol, from its temporary sanctuary in Fort Knox back to Hungary. He confessed that for several weeks before his trip, he had nightmares that the United States had unknowingly harbored a replica instead of the real thing. But all ended well, and the crown today occupies a place of honor in Budapest's national museum.

Hungary's Ambassador to the United Nations, André Erdös, gave an informative and moving overview of recent developments in Central Europe, stressing Hungary's role as a model of stability and his pride in Hungary's increasing responsibility as a member of the Security Council. And finally Hungarian-born author Kati Marton regaled the party with an amusing talk on the lugubrious cast of characters decorating Hungary's paper currency. Her charming finale was a reminder that Hungarians are noted not only for their unusual cuisine and impossible language but also for their sense of humor.

Photographs by Alex McLean

Pancakes à la Gundel (Palacsinta Gundel Módra)

✳

Twelve 6-inch very thin pancakes from your favorite recipe
4 tablespoons butter

Walnut Filling
⅓ cup light cream
½ cup sugar
2 tablespoons light rum
8 ounces walnuts, ground
¼ cup chopped raisins
1 teaspoon grated orange rind

Chocolate-Rum Sauce
4 ounces semisweet chocolate
1 scant cup milk
3 egg yolks
2 tablespoons sugar
2 tablespoons powdered unsweetened cocoa
1 tablespoon butter, melted
2 tablespoons light rum

1. Make the pancakes and set aside until the filling is made.

2. To make the Walnut Filling, bring the cream to a simmer, and add the sugar, rum, walnuts, raisins, and orange rind. Simmer over very low heat for 1 minute. Adjust the texture by adding a little more cream or ground walnuts.

3. Put a heaping teaspoon of filling in the center of each pancake. Fold into quarters instead of rolling.

4. Sauté the folded pancakes in the butter in a large shallow pan for a few minutes on each side. Arrange the pancakes, overlapping, in a warm serving dish.

5. To make the Chocolate-Rum Sauce, melt the chocolate in the milk over low heat. Whip in the egg yolks and remove from heat. Mix in the sugar, cocoa, butter, and rum, and stir until smooth. Adjust the thickness by adding a little more milk if the sauce is too thick to pour.

6. Pour the sauce over the arranged pancakes, and serve at once, 2 pancakes for each serving.

Serves 6

Masterminds of the Hungarian evening huddle together (top). George Lang, left, owner of the much-admired restaurant Café des Artistes in New York and co-owner of the newly restored Cafe Gundel in Budapest, talks with his wife, Jenifer, and fellow Hungarian Paul Kovi, co-owner of New York's renowned Four Seasons restaurant. Author Kati Marton (above), also Hungarian born and a special guest of the evening, is shown here with her husband, newsman Peter Jennings, and her hostess, Budapest-born Vera Blinken.

Café Gundel of Budapest

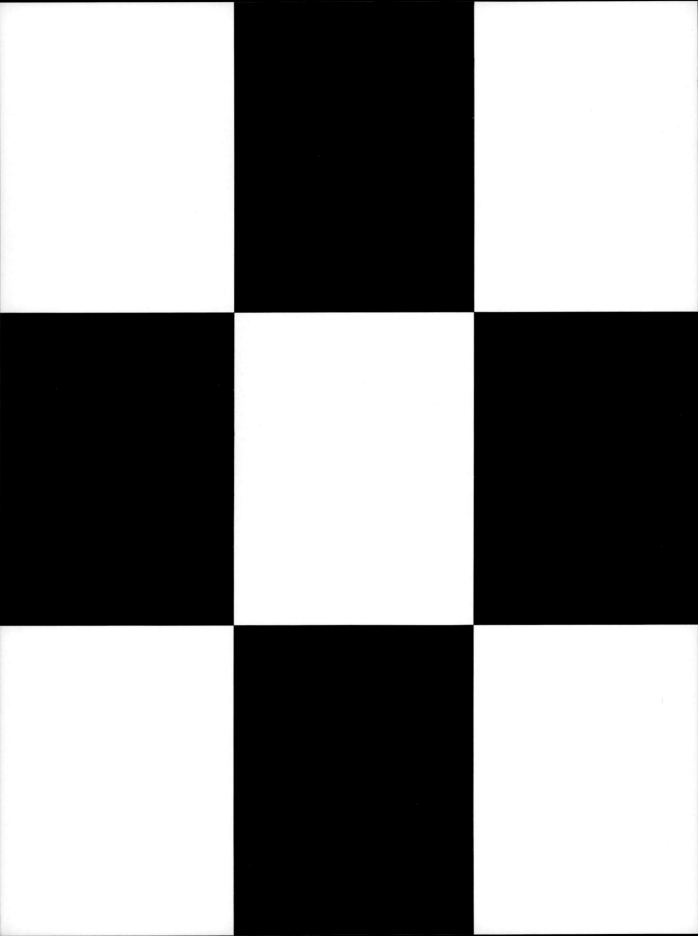

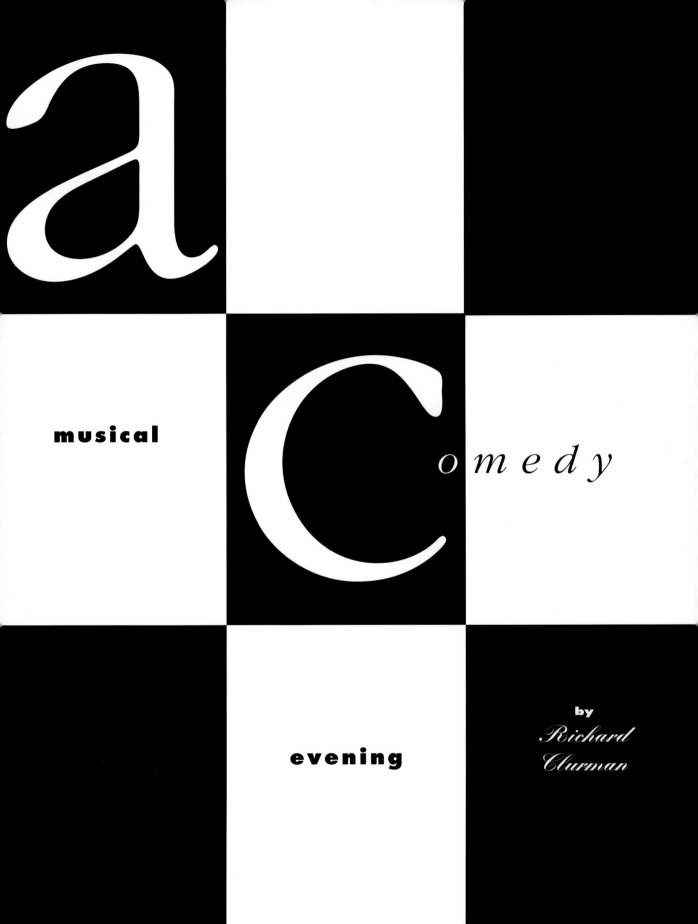

a

musical

Comedy

evening

by
Richard
Clurman

Musical Comedy Evening

Menu

Hors d'Oeuvres
Tiny Cheese Puffs
Crudités
Tiny Sausage Rolls
Stuffed Eggs

Appetizer
Salmon Mousse with Sauce Verte*

Entrée
Loin of Veal with a Bouquet
of Vegetables
Pasta Shells with Parmesan Cheese

Dessert
Profiteroles with Caramel Sauce*

Chassagne-Montrachet Louis Jadot, 1988
Château Lafite-Rothschild, 1983

Chef: Pilar Miguel

*An asterisk denotes that the recipe for the dish is included.

Hostess:

Kitty Carlisle

Hart

The hostess, Kitty Carlisle Hart, chairman of the New York State Council on the Arts, as well as singer, TV personality, and beloved lady about town, welcomes guests to her apartment.

A Musical Comedy Evening

Of the sixty-four beckoning dinner evenings offered on the Library's menu, why was A Musical Comedy Evening with Kitty Hart so oversubscribed? The reason was apparent the minute any one of the twenty-four privileged guests crossed the threshold of her East Sixty-fourth Street apartment. It was Kitty Carlisle Hart herself, with a smile as welcoming as a spring moon, shining on strangers and chums alike. There she is in a long, slim black velvet skirt topped by a chiffon bodice and stole, tastefully adorned with Art Deco sparklers: New York's virtuoso diva of grace, hospitality, and effortless charm.

Never mind that she is, among other things, the chairperson of the New York State Council on the Arts, the recipient of the National Medal of the Arts, and a lifelong performer in the subject of the evening's fete. She is the incomparable Kitty. All else is garnishment.

"It is a very happy evening for me," she says, standing in the curve of the baby grand piano of her living room. "The musical theater is the only art form invented in America." (Jazz aficionados might cavil, but who cares?)

The white and gold doors of her dining room open. Her guests—men in black tie, women in dresses from sequined black and rainbow hues to snowflake white—pass by bowls of coral tulips and alight at three tables for eight, set with her New Orleans grandmother's china and silver. First a chatty meal: salmon mousse, veal with haricot verts, buttered pasta shells overflowing with Parmesan cheese, annealed at the end with caramel-topped profiteroles. Then back to the living room to hear the music of the night.

First a '40s and '50s medley of café and cabaret songs by Ann Hampton Callaway, a lyric soprano out of Chicago on her way to Broadway, singing and giving evidence of Stephen Sondheim's "Being Alive." Then that klieg light of the musical theater, Burton Lane, with a selection of Cole Porter and his and Alan Jay Lerner's *On a Clear Day*. "I wonder," he muses in a question that requires no answer, "how Irving Berlin would have liked rap?" (Berlin's daughter, Elizabeth Peters, was one of the guests.)

Enter Governor Mario Cuomo's wife, announced by the tinkling strains of "Waltzing Matilda." She is embraced by the hostess and by another New Yorker who knows a thing or two about the rigors of public life, Phyllis Wagner, widow of the former New York City mayor and ambassador to Spain.

But the evening itself—the music, the ambience, the warmth of the setting—was the real celebrity.

Photographs by George Whipple

Salmon Mousse
with Sauce Verte

✳

2 pounds fresh salmon

Court Bouillon
3 celery stalks
2 onions, peeled
2 bay leaves
Dash of black pepper
1 teaspoon salt
1 cup white wine

2 envelopes plain gelatin
1 cup sour cream
1 cup mayonnaise
½ teaspoon Tabasco
Juice of 1 large lemon
1 cup tomato juice
Black olives, sliced
Lemon rounds
Cucumber slices
Fresh parsley for garnish

1. Place the salmon and the bouillon ingredients in a large pot, and add enough water to cover the salmon.

2. Bring to a boil and simmer for 15 minutes. Let the bouillon cool.

3. Remove the salmon from the bouillon. Discard the celery, onions, and bay leaves.

4. Soak the gelatin in ½ cup hot water; add to the bouillon.

5. In a food processor blend the salmon, bouillon, sour cream, mayonnaise, Tabasco, lemon juice, and tomato juice. Ladle into a fish mold and chill for several hours, until firm.

6. Unmold the salmon and decorate with slices of black olives for fish eyes, rounds of lemon, and slices of cucumber for gills. Surround with fresh parsley.

Serves 12

While Pilar Miguel, Mrs. Hart's cook, is at the stove, guests including Dick Clurman, left, and Alton Peter mingle in the living room.

Burton Lane, elder statesman of the musical theater (top), entertained guests even
before he went to the piano. Ann Hempton Callaway (above right) sang, but many guests, including Mathilda Cuomo (above left) agreed that the true star of the evening was their hostess,
the Honorable Kitty Carlisle Hart (left).

A Musical Comedy Evening

Profiteroles with Caramel Sauce

✳

1 cup water
1 stick butter
2 teaspoons vanilla extract
1 cup flour
4 eggs
Whipped cream
Apricot jam
½ cup sugar

1. Boil the water; add the butter and vanilla. While the mixture is boiling, add the flour.

2. Remove from the stove and stir the mixture thoroughly. Return the saucepan to the stove and keep over a low flame, stirring thoroughly, until the mixture forms a ball. Remove from the stove and keep stirring the batter, working it well. Add the eggs one by one, beating well.

3. Put the mixture in a pastry bag and form small balls. Bake the balls in a 350°F. oven until golden brown.

4. When baked, cut the balls in half and fill with whipped cream that has a dash of apricot jam in it. You may arrange the filled pastry on a platter to form a pyramid shape.

5. Make a caramel sauce: Combine the sugar in enough water to melt it, and cook until golden brown. Then slightly cool the mixture. For the finishing touch, lace the profiteroles with caramel by spooning the cooled caramel, held up high to form thin strands, in a drizzle pattern over the profiteroles.

The dinner is delightful, the entertainment lively, and author Dick Clurman's toast, below right, a fetching tribute to Kitty.

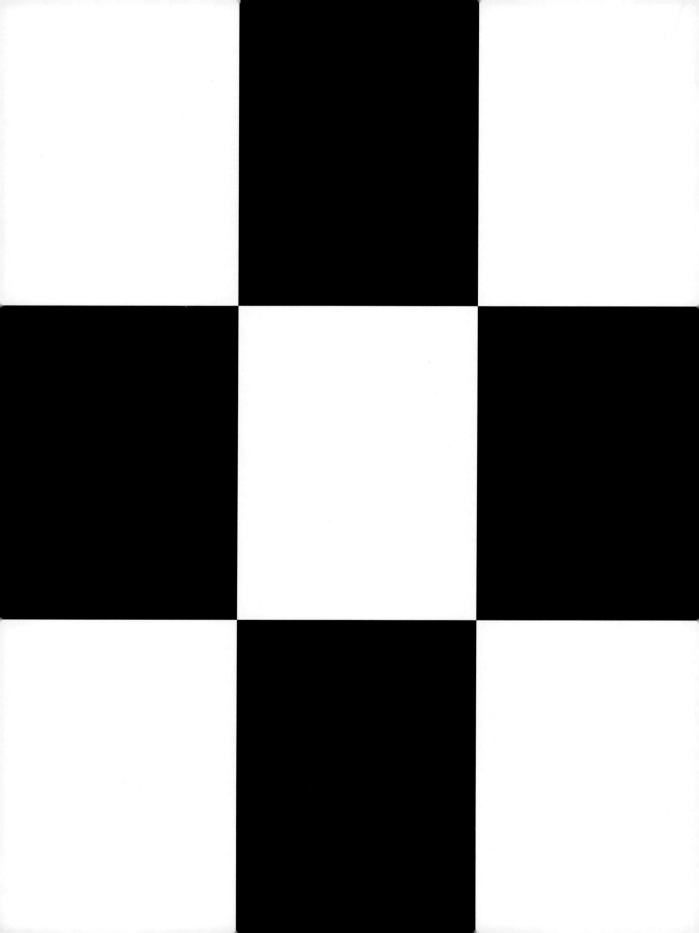

a

rich

and

f amous

dinner

by
*Barbara
Solomon*

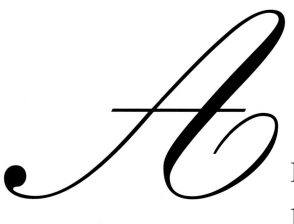

Rich and Famous Dinner

Menu

Appetizers
Curried Tuna Tartare with Pink Radishes
and a Green Celery Sauce

Maine Sea Scallops in Black-Tie*

Entrée
Red Snapper à la Croûte
d'Herbes et Salsifis

Pappardelle Tropézienne*

Dessert
Pomme, Pomme, Pomme*

Soufflé Renversé au Chocolat Amer
et Marmalade d'Orange

Petits Fours et Chocolats

Roederer Cristalle

Chef: Daniel Boulud

Hosts:

Penny Drue Baird

and

Fred Deutsch

*An asterisk denotes that the recipe for the dish is included.

a t the Soho loft of Penny Drue Baird and her husband, Fred Deutsch, the theme was Nobody Knows the Truffles I've Seen. The dinner highlighted the exploits of Robin Leach, master of ceremonies of television's *Lifestyles of the Rich and Famous*, and the culinary skills of Le Cirque's master chef, Daniel Boulud.

This was the third Tables of Content pairing of Penny Baird and Daniel Boulud. In 1987 they put on Les Liaisons Dangereuses, and their tribute to Babar and his fabler Laurent de Brunhoff was the cover story of the 1990 *New York Times* special supplement on gala entertaining.

This year Boulud had the support of Daniele Baliani, his sous-chef at Le Cirque, Jonathan Clark from England, and Frédéric Alexandre from France.

Opulent luxury was apparent when the eighteen black-tie guests entered the dining room, which was tented in gold lamé and filled with princely adornments. The table was dressed in mountains of gold: a central epergne overflowing with glazed grapes and flanked by two candelabra with cascading grapes. Gilded candles in the shape of castles had smaller candled turrets. Treasure chests were filled with candle crowns and candle jewels, and there were stacks of gold-covered chocolate crowns from Fauchon in Paris.

Each place setting had more gold candles in the forms of fleur-de-lis, tassled ottomans, or stacked coins—all from Point à Ligne in Paris. Male guests received gold lamé beggar's purses attached to long gold twigs and filled with Godiva gold chocolates and splits of champagne. Female guests got gold-encrusted scented soaps from parfumière Annik Goutal. The menu offered a feast for kings, and Roederer Cristalle flowed freely throughout the evening.

Conversation was lively and lasted late into the night. Guests, under the direction of emcee Leach, recounted their own lively histories of previous Tables of Content dinners—their personal versions of Lifestyles of the Rich and Famous.

Party photographs by Kevin Lein; still life photographs by Antoine Bootz

A Rich and Famous Dinner

Maine Sea Scallops
in Black-Tie
(Chausson de Saints
Jacques en
Habit Noir)

✳

2 black truffles, fresh or canned, approximately 2 ounces, golf ball size
10 jumbo Maine sea scallops, very fresh and firm
Salt and pepper
8 ounces spinach leaves, cleaned, stems removed
8 ounces puff pastry
1 egg stirred with 1 teaspoon water
1 ounce Noilly-Prat (dry Vermouth)
1 ounce truffle juice
½ cup light chicken stock
1 tablespoon unsalted butter

1. Slice each truffle in 15 thin slices (about 3 per scallop) with a vegetable slicer. Chop the trimmings and set aside for the sauce.

2. Cut each scallop in 4 slices. Rebuild each scallop by alternating 4 slices of scallops with 3 slices of truffle. Season with salt and pepper.

3. Wilt the spinach in a steamer or in hot water for 2 minutes. Drain, cool under cold running water, and drain again. Open each spinach leaf and wrap around each layered scallop (use 1 or 2 leaves per scallop). Set aside.

4. Roll out the puff pastry with a rolling pin until very thin (about ⅛ inch). Cut out 20 disks with a 1½-inch round cookie cutter. Cut out 10 ribbons of puff pastry about 5 inches long and 1½ inches wide. Brush each ribbon with the egg wash. Place 1 scallop side-down on the edge of 1 ribbon and roll the ribbon all the way around the scallop. The edges of the ribbon should overlap to seal the scallop inside. Fold the edges tightly over the top and bottom of the scallop. Brush 2 small disks with the egg wash and place 1 disk on the top and 1 on the bottom of the scallop. Press well to seal. Repeat the same steps to wrap each scallop in the puff pastry.

5. Place the wrapped scallops on a baking pan lined with parchment paper. Brush each scallop lightly with egg wash. Keep refrigerated until ready to cook.

6. Preheat the oven to 450°F. Bake the scallops for 5 to 8 minutes (depending on the size).

7. Reduce the Vermouth to 1 teaspoon. Add the truffle juice and chicken stock. Reduce to ¼ cup and stir in the butter. Add the reserved chopped truffle trimmings. Salt and pepper to taste. Keep warm on the side.

8. Remove the golden scallops from the oven. Split them in half with a sharp knife. Spoon 1 tablespoon of sauce on the bottom of each warm plate. Place 5 scallop halves in a circle on the sauce. Serve warm.

Serves 4

Pappardelle
Tropézienne

✳

You can prepare this recipe in advance. Just cook the pasta right before serving.

½ pound eggplant, peeled and cut into sticks 2 inches long and ¼ inch wide
Zest of 1 lemon, chopped
4 tablespoons olive oil
½ cup finely chopped sweet white onion
1 tablespoon finely chopped garlic (approximately 4 garlic cloves)
⅓ teaspoon dried pimiento flakes
1 yellow sweet pepper (¼ pound), split, cored, and chopped fine
4 large bay leaves
1 pound canned plum tomatoes in tomato juice, drained (set ½ cup juice aside), seeded, and chopped
1 pound fresh tomatoes, peeled, seeded, and chopped fine
Salt
Pinch of sugar
¼ cup black olives (Niçoise), pitted
Fillets of 8 sardines, fresh or canned in oil (see Note)
1 pound pappardelle pasta (wide ribbon pasta), fresh or dried
Pepper
2 sprigs basil

1. Bring 1 quart of water with 1 teaspoon of salt to a boil. Add the eggplant and boil for 2 minutes. Drain, and press the eggplant well to remove all the cooking water. Set aside.

2. Bring 2 cups of water to a boil. Add the lemon zest and boil it for 5 minutes. Drain and reboil the zest in clean water for another 5 minutes. Drain and set aside.

3. Warm 2 tablespoons olive oil in a large kettle over medium heat. Add the onions, garlic, pimiento flakes, sweet pepper, and bay leaves. When the onions are soft and translucent, add the tomatoes (canned and fresh), reserved tomato juice, a touch of salt, and a pinch of sugar, and simmer for 20 minutes. Add the eggplant and black olives and cook for another 10 to 20 minutes. Add the lemon zest. Taste the sauce, discard the bay leaves, and adjust the seasoning if needed.

4. Bring 4 quarts of water with 2 table-spoons of salt to a boil. (It will be used to cook the pasta just before serving.)

5. Warm ½ tablespoon olive oil in a nonstick pan over high heat. Season the sardine fillets, and sear them on the skin side for 1 minute. Turn them over and keep warm on the side.

6. Cook the pappardelle until just tender, 4 minutes if fresh, 8 minutes if dried. Stir from time to time. Drain, and toss with 1 tablespoon olive oil, salt, and pepper.

7. Place the pappardelle on the bottom of a warm dish. Cover with the sauce. Arrange the sardine fillets in a fan shape on the top, and decorate with basil leaves. Sprinkle with the remaining ½ tablespoon of olive oil. Serve on warm plates.

Note: If you are using canned sardines instead of fresh, don't cook them. Just add them on top of the pasta.

Serves 4

Pomme, Pomme, Pomme

✳

This recipe combines apple sherbet, apple salad, and caramelized apples to make a luscious, impressive-looking dessert.

10 McIntosh apples (medium size)
Juice of 1 lemon
10 tablespoons granulated sugar (5 ounces)
1 cup water
1 tablespoon confectioners' sugar

1. Make the sherbet: Peel 7 apples. Split, core, and toss them with half the lemon juice. Crush the apples in a juice extractor. Stir 5 tablespoons granulated sugar into the juice and pour into a sherbet machine. Run until it is of firm consistency. Remove from the sherbet machine and put into the freezer. Keep frozen until needed. Reserve the apple pulp.

2. Make the apple salad: Mix the apple pulp with 1 cup water and the remaining lemon juice. Add 4 tablespoons granulated sugar. Bring to a boil. Boil for 2 minutes. Strain and cool. Set aside. Peel, split, and core 2 apples. Cut them into thin slices and add them to the apple syrup.

3. Make the caramelized apple: Preheat the oven to 325°F. Peel, core, and cut the apple into very thin slices (about 16 rings) with a vegetable cutter. Place each ring on a nonstick baking pan or parchment paper. Bake the rings briefly until light brown. Sprinkle them with confectioners' sugar and glaze them under the broiler. Remove and let cool. Keep them in the freezer until needed.

4. To present: In a prefrozen bowl, arrange the sliced apples in the syrup like a flower on the bottom (overlapping the slices from the edge of the bowl to the center). Add 2 tablespoons apple syrup. Place a ball of apple sherbet in the center. Decorate with the caramelized apple pushed lightly into the sherbet.

Serves 4

Under a golden tent, the dining table groans with gold, gold, and more gold:
The centerpiece is of gilded grapes; golden castles are really golden candles; golden satchels filled
with golden treasures are at each place; and golden coins—chocolates from Fauchon in Paris—
are flung in artful abandon the length of the table. A dinner that more than lived up
to its name—all that glittered really was gold on this occasion.

Tables of Content

appendix

Volunteer Hosts and Hostesses

On these pages is a list of all the hosts and hostesses who have volunteered to give Tables of Content dinners for the Library during the last decade. A close study of the list will reveal those who have volunteered to give all six dinners.

Tuesday, December 6, 1983

Mr. and Mrs. Sam Aaron
Ms. Andree Abramoff
Mr. and Mrs. Andrew A.
Anspach
Harley Baldwin
Mr. and Mrs. Michael
Batterberry
Joseph Baum
James Beard
Mr. and Mrs. Peter Bienstock
Marian and Donald Burros
Dr. and Mrs. Luis Casas
Irena Chalmers
Craig Claiborne
Mrs. Phyllis Collins
Vivian Collyer
Mr. and Mrs. Sydney Cone III
Barbara Conwell
Mr. and Mrs. Edward
Costikyan

Maxime de la Falaise
Mr. and Mrs. Jean Delmas
Mr. and Mrs. Georges de
Menil
Mr. and Mrs. Joel S.
Ehrenkranz
Mr. and Mrs. Donald Elliott
Robert Ellsworth
Mr. and Mrs. Ahmet H.
Ertegun
Mr. and Mrs. Bruce R. Farkas
Mr. and Mrs. Arthur A. Feder
Mr. and Mrs. Lawrence A.
Fleischman
Mr. and Mrs. Anastassios
Fondaras
Christopher Forbes
Betty Friedan
Dr. and Mrs. Edwin Gee
Mrs. Geraldine Stutz Gibbs
Dr. Wendy Gimbel
Arthur Gold and Robert
Fizdale
Mrs. John D. Gordan
Mr. and Mrs. Robert D. Graff
Gael Greene
Dr. and Mrs. Vartan Gregorian
Tom Guinzburg
Mr. and Mrs. Hugh Hardy
Mr. and Mrs. Conrad Harper
Marcella and Victor Hazan
Mr. and Mrs. Andrew Heiskell
Moira Hodgson
Jati Hoon
Mrs. Robert Hufstader

Mr. and Mrs. Philip Isles
Mr. and Mrs. John Jakobson
Ms. Barbara Kafka
Mr. and Mrs. Nicholas de B.
Katzenbach
Mr. and Mrs. Stephen E.
Kaufman
Nancy, Lady Keith
Dr. and Mrs. Ed King
Mr. and Mrs. Robert Kirsch
Mr. and Mrs. John
Klingenstein
Paul Kovi
Mr. and Mrs. Frank Lalli
Jenifer and George Lang
Wendy Larsen
Stephen Lash
Mr. and Mrs. Daniel J. Leab
Kay and Warner LeRoy
Mrs. William Lewis
Mr. and Mrs. Leon Lianides
Ellen and Arthur Liman
Mr. and Mrs. John V. Lindsay
Mr. and Mrs. Robert Lindsay
Diane Love
Sirio Maccioni
Mr. and Mrs. David Mahoney
Mr. and Mrs. Francis S.
Mason, Jr.
Robert Mayzen and Roger
Fessaguet
Mr. and Mrs. Peter Meltzer
Mr. and Mrs. Maurice Moore
Mr. and Mrs. Lester Morse
Helen and Jack Nash

Mr. and Mrs. Donald
  Newhouse
Mike and Annabel Nichols
Mr. and Mrs. Alan Pakula
Mr. and Mrs. Richard
  Pasculano
Mr. and Mrs. Carl H.
  Pforzheimer III
Madeline Polcy
Mr. and Mrs. Leon Polsky
Mr. and Mrs. William Rayner
Mr. and Mrs. Samuel P. Reed
John Connors and William
  Rice
Richard and Carole Rifkind
Mr. and Mrs. Daniel Rose
Mr. and Mrs. David S. Rose
Mr. and Mrs. Marshall Rose
Mr. and Mrs. Alfred A.
  Rosenberg
Mr. and Mrs. Peter J.
  Rosenwald
Colette and James Rossant
Mrs. John Barry Ryan
Mr. and Mrs. Richard Salomon
Mr. and Mrs. David Saltonstall
Jeanette Watson Sanger
Francine Scherer
Mr. and Mrs. Richardson
  Scurry, Jr.
Wilfrid Sheed
Mr. and Mrs. Howard Sloan
Ruth and Harvey Spear
Mr. and Mrs. Paul Steindler
Mr. and Mrs. Alfred Stern
Mr. and Mrs. Fred Mustard
  Stewart
Martha Stewart
David Stickelber
Mr. and Mrs. Myron K. Stone
Mr. and Mrs. Harold Tanner
Mr. and Mrs. Walter Thayer

Calvin Trillin
Mrs. Helen S. Tucker
Mr. and Mrs. Louis Tyrrell
Miriam Ungerer
Alfred Viazzi
Mr. and Mrs. C. Carter Walker
Shelby White and Leon Levy
Jane and Michael Whiteman
Mr. and Mrs. Lester
  Wunderman
Mr. and Mrs. Roger Yaseen
Mr. and Mrs. Daniel A. Zilkha
Mr. and Mrs. Eugene I. Zuriff

Tuesday,
December 10, 1985

Michael Aaron
Alice Allen
Lilly Auchincloss
Felice and David Axelrod
Penny Baird and Kenneth
  Alpert
Mr. and Mrs. Donald
  Beckwith
Peter Bienstock
Marie Brenner and Ernest
  Pomerantz
Mr. and Mrs. David C.
  Brodhead
Sybil and Bill Broyles
Marian and Donald Burros
Ann and Larry Buttenwieser
Craig Claiborne
Irene and Philip Clark
Betsy and Alan Cohn
Barbara and Edward
  Costikyan
Mrs. Mary Sharp Cronson
Mr. and Mrs. Clive Cummis
Mrs. Catherine Curran
Peggy and Dick Danziger

Mr. and Mrs. Nathaniel de
  Rothschild
Barbaralee Diamonstein and
  Carl Spielvogel
Sean Driscoll
Barbara F. Duke
Osborn and Inger McCabe
  Elliott
Ms. Joni Evans and Mr.
  Richard Snyder
Meryle and Martin Evans
Mr. and Mrs. Thomas Mellon
  Evans
Florence and Richard
  Fabricant
Elizabeth and Lee Falk
Mr. and Mrs. Bruce Farkas
Mr. and Mrs. Jonathan Farkas
Mr. and Mrs. Arthur Feder
Mr. and Mrs. Lawrence A.
  Fleischman
Mr. and Mrs. Christopher
  Forbes
Mr. and Mrs. Roger Friedman
Wendy Gimbel
Elinor Giobbi
Toni and Jim Goodale
Mrs. John D. Gordan
Jamee and Peter Gregory
Lee Guber and Lois Wyse
  Guber
Mr. and Mrs. Mark Hampton
Tiziana and Hugh Hardy
Mr. and Mrs. Richard V. Hare
Marcella and Victor Hazan
Don and Marilyn Hewitt
Mr. and Mrs. James Hoge
Gene Hovis
Mrs. Robert Hufstader
Mr. and Mrs. James H.
  Kabler III
Barbara Kafka

Nadine Kalachnikoff

Elizabeth and Barrett Kalb

Susan and Howard Kaminsky

Mr. and Mrs. Robert Kirsch

Mr. and Mrs. John
   Klingenstein

Mr. and Mrs. Peter Krulewitch

Mr. Peter Kump

Carole and Frank Lalli

Evelyn and Leonard Lauder

Joanne Lazar

Mr. and Mrs. Samuel LeFrak

Mr. and Mrs. Ronald J. Lenney

Warner and Kay LeRoy

Wendy and Hugh Levey

Mr. and Mrs. Richard Lewine

Eileen Yin-Fei Lo and Fred
   Ferretti

Ms. Susan Loren

Frances and Bob Low

Mr. and Mrs. Lester Morse

Mr. William E. Murray

Helen and Jack Nash

Susan and Donald Newhouse

Mrs. Jan Cushing Olympitis

Hannah and Alan Pakula

Mr. and Mrs. David B. Pall

Mr. and Mrs. Leon B. Polsky

Warrie and James Price

Joanna Pruess

Harvey and Françoise
   Rambach

Mrs. Marjorie Anne Reed

Dr. Richard and Carole
   Rifkind

Mrs. Eisen Rinzler

Daniel and Joanna S. Rose

Mr. and Mrs. Marshall Rose

Judy and Alfred Rosenberg

Mr. and Mrs. Stephen M. Ross

Berton and Katherine
   Roueché

Mr. Thomas O. Ryder

Julie Sahni

Dr. and Mrs. Nathan E. Saint-
   Amand

Mr. and Mrs. David Saltonstall

Joan and Arthur Sarnoff

Jean-Michel Savoca and
   Boyce Brawley

Fern and Tennyson Schad

Alexandra and Arthur
   Schlesinger

Mr. and Mrs. Herbert S.
   Schlosser

Mrs. Sarah Schulte

Pamela and Richard Scurry

Melissa and Patrick Séré

Mr. and Mrs. Benjamin
   Shute, Jr.

Bonnie and Stephen Simon

Anita and Neal Slavin

Sonny and Howard Sloan

Jean and Steve Smith

Mr. and Mrs. Stephen Spahn

Mr. and Mrs. Robert Steinberg

Mr. and Mrs. Fred Mustard
   Stewart

Mr. and Mrs. Myron K. Stone

Helen and George Studley

Peter G. Terian

Mr. and Mrs. Michael M.
   Thomas

Barbara and Donald Tober

Jeremiah Tower

George Trescher

Mrs. Helen S. Tucker

Mr. and Mrs. Senen Ubina

Julia and Carter Walker

Jeannette Watson

Pam Hill and Tom Wicker

Mr. and Mrs. Roger Yaseen

Kevin Zraly

Mr. and Mrs. Eugene Zuriff

Tuesday,
December 8, 1987

Mona Riklis Ackerman

Ken Aretsky

Penny Baird and Kenneth
   Alpert

Wayne C. Batcheler

Michael and Ariane
   Batterberry

Jim and Keven Bellows

Mr. and Mrs. Francis Belmont

Mr. and Mrs. Thornton F.
   Bradshaw

Thomas and Anne Bennett
   Brandenburger

Eleanor and Richard Brenner

Marie Brenner and Ernie
   Pomerantz

Mr. and Mrs. David C.
   Brodhead

Marian and Donald Burros

Ms. Giosetta Capriati

Mrs. Anne Cox Chambers

Mr. and Mrs. Edward T. Chase

Craig Claiborne

Mr. Mario d'Urso

Mr. Richard Ekstract

Karen and Alfonso Escalera

Laura Evans

Joseph Famularo

Mimi and Richard Fischbein

Mr. and Mrs. Christopher
   Forbes

Mary Gilliatt

Mrs. Paula Gilpatric

Edmund and Leslie Glass

Jessica Goldberg

Mr. and Mrs. James Goodale

Mr. and Mrs. William O.
   Harbach

Phillips Hathaway

Mrs. Emi Heater

Pam Hill and Tom Wicker

Mr. and Mrs. James Hoge

June and Dan Jenkins

Gillian Jolis and Andrew
Goldstein

Jennifer Dodge Josselson

Ferne Kadish

Barbara Kafka

Arden Kahlo

Barrett and Betsy Kalb

Susan and Howard Kaminsky

Mr. and Mrs. John Karlton

Rona and Robert Kiley

Mr. and Mrs. John
Klingenstein

Sarah and Victor Kovner

Mr. and Mrs. Henry Kravis

Peter Krueger

Deborah and Peter
Krulewitch

Peter Kump and Nicholas
Malgieri

Carole and Frank Lalli

Doe Lang

Joanne D. Lazar

Isabelle Leeds

Mr. and Mrs. Robert Lenzner

Warner and Kay LeRoy

Mr. and Mrs. Hugh Levey

Bob and Frances Low

Sheila and Richard Lukins

Hermes Mallea

Carey Maloney

Zarela Martinez

Jane Montant and Gerald
Asher

Mr. and Mrs. Lester Morse

Mr. and Mrs. Bill Moyers

The Consul-General and Mrs.
Pascal Alan Nazareth

Mr. and Mrs. Donald
Newhouse

Mr. and Mrs. William A.
Newman

Dr. and Mrs. Winfred
Overholser

Mr. and Mrs. Edward D.
Pardoe III

Mr. and Mrs. Steven Park

Jane and David Parshall

Mr. and Mrs. Charles D.
Peebler

Mr. and Mrs. Gifford Phillips

Mr. and Mrs. Leon B. Polsky

Mr. George Prifti

Robert and Peggy Hill
Rosenkranz

Anne Rosenzweig

Nancy and Stephen Ross

Julie Sahni

Mr. and Mrs. John T. Sargent

Mr. and Mrs. Arthur Sarnoff

Mr. and Mrs. Herbert S.
Schlosser

MaryJo Schwalbach and Ira
Gitler

Mr. and Mrs. Richardson G.
Scurry, Jr.

Susan Seidel

Mr. and Mrs. Frederick R.
Selch

Bobbie Seril

Paul Sinclaire

Mr. and Mrs. Donald Siskind

Mr. and Mrs. Howard Sloan

Captain and Mrs. Roland B.
Stearns

Mr. and Mrs. Alfred Stern

Mr. and Mrs. Fred Mustard
Stewart

Mr. and Mrs. Donald B. Straus

Mr. Terry Terhune

Barbara and Allen Thomas

Donald and Barbara Tober

Mr. and Mrs. Marvin S. Traub

Mr. and Mrs. Robert Trump

Mr. and Mrs. John Veronis

Mr. Gordon Wallace

Alexander M. Ward

Jacqueline Bograd Weld and
Matthew Weld

William Wilkinson

Chuck Williams

Mortimer Zuckerman

Mr. and Mrs. Eugene Zuriff

Tuesday, December 5, 1989

Kenneth Alpert and Claire
Deutsch

Jean Bach

Penny Baird and Freddy
Deutsch

Patricia Bradshaw

Boyce A. Brawley and Jean-
Michel Savoca

Carol and Emil Brock

Nancie and David Brodhead

Dawn Bryan

Marian and Donald Burros

Mr. and Mrs. Nathaniel de
Rothschild

Beth and James DeWoody

Richard Ekstract

Miss Laura Evans

Sylvain V. Fareri

Kimberly Farkas

Mr. and Mrs. Matthew S.
Farkas

Ms. Christy Ferer

Mimi and Richard Fischbein

Marilyn Friedman and
Thomas Block

Neal Gabler

Mr. and Mrs. John Bristol
Glass, Jr.

Faith Golding

Sondra and Celso Gonzalez-
Falla

Mr. and Mrs. James Goodale

Beverly Sills Greenough and
Peter Greenough

Fay Harbach

Marife Hernandez

Mr. and Mrs. Elie Hirschfeld

Sharon and Jim Hoge

Gene Hovis

Katharine Johnson

Mr. and Mrs. John Karlton

Mr. and Mrs. William
Kinsolving

Mr. and Mrs. William T.
Knowles

Deborah and Peter
Krulewitch

Yara Labal

Carole and Frank Lalli

Doe Lang

Mr. and Mrs. Stephen Lash

Mr. and Mrs. Hugh Levey

Judy Licht and Jerry Della
Femina

Mr. and Mrs. Robert A. Low

Mr. and Mrs. Norton W.
Mailman

Hermes Mallea

Carey Maloney

Zarela Martinez

Jack and Mary Lou Masey

Mrs. Mark Millard

Grace Mirabella and Bill
Cahan

Mr. and Mrs. Stephen Miron

Gianfranco Monacelli

Jane Montant and Gerald
Asher

Mr. and Mrs. Rupert Murdoch

Mr. and Mrs. Cyril Naphegyi

Susan and Donald Newhouse

Mr. and Mrs. Stuart Oran

Mr. and Mrs. Edward D.
Pardoe III

Patricia Patterson

Mr. and Mrs. Charles Peebler

Susan and Elihu Rose

Julie Sahni

Mr. and Mrs. John Sargent

Madame Eliane Scali

Fern and Tennyson Schad

Joan Blackett Schlank

Sara Lee and Axel Schupf

Pamela and Richard Scurry

Susan Seidel

Vishwa and Pallavi Shah

Paul Sinclaire

Beth and Donald Siskind

Suzanne Slesin

Mr. and Mrs. Howard Sloan

Ellen and Lawrence Sosnow

Mr. and Mrs. Donald A.
Sperling

Mr. and Mrs. John Stark

Michael Steinberg

Margaret Stern

Mr. and Mrs. Fred Mustard
Stewart

Jane Susskind-Narins

Amanda Urban and Ken
Auletta

Mr. and Mrs. Gerald van der
Kemp

Mrs. Alexander Orr Vietor

Mr. and Mrs. Richard A. Voell

Mr. and Mrs. Michael
Whiteman

Mr. Robert C. Woolley and
Mr. Michael Meehan

*Wednesday, December 11,
1991*

Ken Aretsky

Penny Baird and Fred
Deutsch

Dr. and Mrs. Daniel Baker

Mr. Charles B. Benenson and
Mrs. Jane Stein

Vera and Donald Blinken

Patricia Bradshaw

Lily Brett and David Rankin

Mr. and Mrs. David C.
Brodhead

Cynthia and Edward Brodsky

Grace and Bill Cahan

Virginia and Peter Carry

The Honorable Anne Cox
Chambers

Craig Claiborne

Hildy Parks and Alexander H.
Cohen

Barbara and Edward
Costikyan

Joan and Joe Cullman

Mr. and Mrs. Lewis Cullman

Ronnie Davis

Mr. and Mrs. Daniel P.
Davison

Mr. and Mrs. Nathaniel de
Rothschild

Peter Duchin and Brooke
Hayward

Eileen and Richard Ekstract

Florence and Richard
Fabricant

Mr. and Mrs. Jonathan Farkas

Ms. Christy Ferer

Mr. and Mrs. Timothy Forbes

Marilyn Friedman and
Thomas Block

Barry Michael Gaines, M.D.

Geraldine Stutz Gibbs
Toni and Jamie Goodale
Mr. and Mrs. David Granger
Mr. and Mrs. Marco Grassi
Kathy and Alan Greenberg
Beverly Sills Greenough and
    Peter Greenough
Harriet and Alan Gruber
Louise and Henry Grunwald
Sir David and Lady Hannay
The Honorable Kitty Carlisle
    Hart
Marian and Andrew Heiskell
Pam Hill and Tom Wicker
Nancy Hoffman and Peter
    Greenwald
Sharon and Jim Hoge
Katharine Johnson and
    William Rayner
Gillian Jolis and Andrew
    Goldstein
Isobel and Ronald Konecky
Susan and David Kraus
Deborah and Peter
    Krulewitch
Carole and Frank Lalli
Warner and Kay LeRoy
Wendy and Hugh Levey
Ellen and Arthur Liman
Frances and Robert Low
Joshua Mack and Ron Warren
Mr. and Mrs. Norton W.
    Mailman
James Marlas and Marie
    Nugent-Head
Zarela Martinez
Mr. and Mrs. Walter
    Maynard, Jr.
Joanie and Terry McDonell
Mary McFadden
Harvey M. and Lois Wyse
    Meyerhoff

Abby and Howard Milstein
Peter and Cathy Morrell
Roberta Morrell
Mr. and Mrs. Carl Mueller
Susan and Donald Newhouse
Mr. and Mrs. William A.
    Newman
Nancy and John Novogrod
Hannah and Alan Pakula
Patricia S. Patterson
Toni and Chuck Peebler
Dounia Rathbone
Eugenia Rawls
Roxana and Hamilton
    Robinson
Elizabeth and Felix Rohatyn
Mr. and Mrs. Andrew Rosen
Julie Sahni
Gene and Keren Saks
Fern and Tennyson Schad
Pamela and Richard Scurry
Judith Segal
Mr. and Mrs. Frederick R.
    Selch
Gil Shiva
Paul Sinclaire
Beth and David Siskind
Sonny Sloan
Jeanette Solomon and Peter J.
    Solomon
Ann and Paul Sperry
Francesca Stanfill and Peter
    Tufo
Domna and Frank Stanton
Mr. and Mrs. John Stark
Mr. and Mrs. Fred Mustard
    Stewart
Faith Stewart-Gordon
Charles and Mary Tanenbaum
Mrs. Jeanne Thayer
Marchesa Katrin Theodoli

Mr. and Mrs. Alan V. Tishman
The Hon. and Mrs. John Train
Alice and Calvin Trillin
Joan Vass
Vera Wang and Arthur Becker
Matthew and Jacqueline
    Bograd Weld
Angela Westwater
Robert Woolley
Gail Zweigenthal and Gerald
    Asher

Special Guests and Chefs for 1991 Dinners

Each dinner is traditionally graced by one or more Special Guests who donate their services to enhance the evening. Chefs, speakers, singers, authors, composers, actors, and actresses have all contributed their talents. Here is the list of Special Guests for 1991.

Ken Auletta
Paul Balfour
Daniel Boulud (chef)
Carolyn Brady
Robert Brubaker
Susan Caldwell
Joseph A. Califano, Jr.
Penelope and Luis Casas
    (chef)
Dick Cavett
Julia Child
Tom Clancy
Judy Collins
Quentin Crisp
Matilda Cuomo
Ariane Daguin (chef)

Eric DeCamps
Mayor and Mrs. Dinkins
E. L. Doctorow
Chancellor Joseph A.
　Fernandez
Geraldine Fitzgerald
Robert Fizdale
Larry Forgione (chef)
Gwynne Geyer
Marshall Goldman and Merle
　Goldman
George Goodman (Adam
　Smith)
Sharon Graham
Michael Graves
Francine Duplessix Gray
Cynthia Gregory
George Grizzard
John Guare
Jessica Hagedorn
David Halberstam
Cynthia Harris
Ted Hartley
Oscar Hijuelos
Geoffrey Holder
Gene Hovis
Alice Hudson
Anne Jacson
Barbara Kafka
Christopher Keene
Richard Kiley
Jeffrey Kneebone
Paul Kovi
Burton Lane
George Lang
Robin Leach
Christopher Lehmann-Haupt
Jerome Lowenthal
John M. Lundquist

Kati Marton
Christopher Mason
Jay McInerney
John McLaughlin
Richard Meier
Dina Merrill
Ted Morgan
Frederic Morton
Consul General Alonso
　Munoz
Gloria Naylor
LeRoy Neiman
P. J. O'Rourke
Robert M. Parker Jr.
Bert Parks
Estelle Parsons
George Plimpton
Anthony Quinn
Jason Robards
Andy Rooney
Robert Rosenblum
Anne Rosenzweig (chef)
David Roth
Dick Schaap
Simon Schama
Philip Setzer
Bobby Short
Mark Strausman (chef)
Elaine Stritch
Gay Talese
Billy Taylor
Michael M. Thomas
Calvin Tomkins
Marcia Tucker
Michael Valenti
Susan Vogel
Eli Wallach
Eileen Weinberg (chef)
Barry and Susan Wine (chef)

Tuesday,
December 7, 1993

Ariel and Michael
Corice and Armand Arman
Gerald Asher
Dr. Penny Drue Baird and
　Mr. Fred Deutsch
Jennifer Bartlett
Robert Glenn Bernbaum
Marilyn Friedman and
　Thomas Block
Anne Cox Chambers
Craig Claiborne
Heather Cohane
Dorothy and Lewis Cullman
Mr. and Mrs. Joseph Cullman
Hon. Benoit d'Aboville,
　Ministry Plenipotentiary,
　Consul General of France
Gabriella DeFerrari and
　Raymond Learsey
William H. Donaldson
　and New York Stock
　Exchange, Inc.
Mr. and Mrs. Richard Ekstract
Mr. and Mrs. Peter Eliel
Tina Brown and Harold Evans
Florence and Richard
　Fabricant
Mimi and Richard Fischbein
Mr. and Mrs. Timothy C.
　Forbes
Anne and Alain Goldrach
Mr. and Mrs. James C.
　Goodale
Mr. and Mrs. David Granger
Great Performances
　Caterers, Inc.
Mr. and Mrs. Alan Greenberg

Georgia Shreve Greenberg
    and Glenn H. Greenberg
Alexis Gregory
Mr. and Mrs. Mark Hampton
Sir David and Lady Hannay
Phillips Hathaway and
    Sotheby's, Inc.
Andrew and Marian Heiskell
Mr. and Mrs. James Hoge
Mr. and Mrs. John Jakobson
Morton Janklow
Mr. and Mrs. John Klingenstein
Deborah and Peter Krulewitch
Barbara and Richard Lane
Lionel Larner
Wendy and Hugh Levey
Louis.
Jean Bronson Mahoney
Mr. and Mrs. Norton W.
    Mailman
Hermes Mallea
Carey Maloney
Jane and Peter Marino
Mr. and Mrs. Walter
    Maynard, Jr.
Joanie and Terry McDonell
Marian McEvoy
Caroline Rennolds Milbank
    and Jeremiah Milbank
Mr. and Mrs. Howard Milstein
Mr. and Mrs. Lester S.
    Morse, Jr.
Senga Mortimer
Charles and Susan
    Calhoun Moss
Mr. and Mrs. Donald
    Newhouse

Mr. and Mrs. Edward D.
    Pardoe III
Mrs. Patricia S. Patterson
Mr. and Mrs. Charles D.
    Peebler, Jr.
Helen Pratt
Frank and Jeanne Prial
Mr. and Mrs. William Rayner
Joan Rivers
Jonathan and Jeannette Rosen
Mr. and Mrs. A. M. Rosenthal
Mr. and Mrs. Renny Saltzman
Fern and Tennyson Schad
Pamela and Richard Scurry, Jr.
Muriel F. Siebert
Sonny Sloan
Ellen and Lawrence Sosnow
Martha Stewart
John and Jane Stubbs
The Honorable and
    Mrs. John Train
Jean H. Vanderbilt
Katherine Whiteside
Pam Hill and Tom Wicker
Robert C. Woolley
Lois Robbins Zaro and
    Andrew Zaro
Ms. Gail Zweigenthal

Complete as of printing

index